MGNREGA

Success or Failure!

MGNREGA

Success or Failure!

Moitri Dey

ADROIT

Adroit Publishers

New Delhi

ISBN : 978-81-87393-07-8

First Published in 2021

Published by
ADROIT PUBLISHERS
4675/21, Ganpati Bhawan, Ansari Road,
Daryaganj, New Delhi-110 002
Phone : 011-23266030

Distributors
AKHIL BOOK DISTRIBUTORS
email: akhilbooks@yahoo.com
akhilbks@gmail.com

Typesetting—Gaurav Graphices, Delhi-110094
E-mail: gauravsingh1908@gmail.com
Printed at: Avantika Printers Private Limited.

Dedicated to

My Darling Daughter, Aanya

CONTENT

Foreword

Dr. Moitri Dey's book on *MGNREGA Success or Failure!* is based on her doctoral research of MGNREGA in four districts of Rajasthan. Implementation studies of government programmes of the scale and nature of MGNREGA can give much needed feedback and useful insights to policy makers in order to implement mid course corrections, if necessary. The Right based system of governance started in India in the first decade of the 21st century with the Right to Information Act 2005 and the National Rural Employment Guarantee Act, 2005. Today, MGNREGA is the largest social sector (wage employment) programme in the world and therefore its impacts in the world's largest democracy need to be studied very carefully. Implementation research is not very strong in India; therefore Moitri's study is timely and relevant. The sheer magnitude of the effort in providing employment for 100 days to every rural citizen in 29 states of India besides the number of people involved in execution and the claims made on policy makers by intended beneficiaries, itself calls for a systematic inquiry into related issues of accountability and citizen centric governance. How and to what extent the Right based approach to governance has empowered our citizens and what shortcomings exist in the implementation of the Act, are the central concerns of this book.

Moitri's book rests on extensive data based on field work and the reason for contrasting 2 districts which are "successful implementers" with the other 2 viewed as "laggards" is to understand the problems of implementation on a pan Indian scale. There are enormous variations in implementing even government flagship programmes like the MGNREGA is a fact, which policymakers have come to acknowledge.

An Employment Guarantee Act provides a universal and enforceable legal right to the most basic form of employment. The enactment of the Act was symptomatic of India's efforts to move from being a "procedural" democracy to a "substantivist" one. The real essence of the Act rests in its uniform application in 29 states of India. However, the essence of citizenship lies in giving every rural citizen an equal basic entitlement as a guaranteed right. Moitri's research raises very important questions for policy makers and all others interested in administrative and development studies in a multi-layered democracy like India.

Rumki Basu
Professor of Public Administration
Department of Political Science
Jamia Millia Islamia

ACKNOWLEDGEMENT

I would like to thank my father who taught me to dream big. It is his blessing which gave me courage and strength to withstand all the difficulties I faced during the course of this book. I am thankful to the Almighty for his blessings which have helped me to complete the book.

I cannot find words to express my sincere gratitude to Professor Rumki Basu. Without her academic excellence, patience and encouragement, this book would not have been possible. She has been very supportive and inspiring. I will always remain indebted to her.

This book would not have been possible without the help of several individuals who in one way or another contributed and extended their valuable assistance in the preparation and completion of this study. I acknowledge the support provided by various people in Rajasthan. I would like to thank all those who have helped in the data collection of the study.

I owe my deepest gratefulness to my family particularly my husband, Tushar who has been my motivation as I hurdle all the obstacles in the completion of the book. A special thanks to Dr. Sarish Sebastian for his help at any point of time. I am also grateful to Mr. Akhil Sharma, Adroit Publishers who has been very patient all through the course.

MOITRI DEY
2016

PREFACE

The book is an outcome of my doctoral research on implementation of MGNREGA in Rajasthan. Implementation is one of the primary components in the policy making process. It is the active constituent of the process, thereby making it one of the most important pivots of policymaking. However, implementation study never received appropriate attention from the early scholars of policy studies. It has also been seen that there is a gap between policy formation and its expected outcome i.e. its implementation. Implementation studies have a short history which means that there is lack of extensive study of implementation of policies. Moreover, the implementation studies carried so far are West-oriented which leaves less scope for its applicability in other countries particularly in the developing and under-developing countries. A successful implementation of a programme depends on a strong, well defined and systematically analysed policy. At the end of the twentieth century, study of implementation started to expand and develop. The works explored the process of policy implementation and made a clear distinction between policy formulation and implementation. However, the pertinent issue in the study of implementation of public policy remains the same. It continues to focus on the issue of gaps between policy formation and its implementation, which leads to unsuccessful implementation of policy.

The problems in policy implementation are more prominent in the Third World countries. Since most of the Third World finds itself lack in infrastructure, finance, expert personnel, etc., a policy might not be as successful as those implemented in First World countries. Generally speaking, the policies in Western countries are incremental in nature. The concerns of the policies remain the same with little changes in the policy design. However, most Third World countries have recently started with the development process, and their limited resources leave less scope for such incremental policies. Thus, implementation of a policy is of utmost importance.

Similarly in India, there is a lack of proper implementation of public policies. There is no systematic detailed analysis of policy before it is made and implemented. It is the Planning Commission which works as a core policy institution and plans for the socio-economic development of the country. So planning and policy making are treated equally. There is no proper policy analysis done when policy decisions are made. This ultimately leads to a faulty policy design and unsuccessful policy implementation. There is a need of a separate body comprising of experts in policy analysis to carry out policy studies in India.

Based on the above context, the book would look at the implementation of the MGNREGA in Rajasthan. The Indian Government passed the Mahatma Gandhi National Rural Employment Guarantee Act in September, 2005 and launched the Mahatma Gandhi National Rural Employment Guarantee Programme on February 2, 2006. The Act guarantees the right to work by providing 100 days of guaranteed wage employment in a financial year to every rural household whose adult members are willing to do unskilled manual work. The enactment of the Act was a major achievement for Indian democracy. However, the real essence of the Act lies in its successful implementation of the Act. The study intends to answer some of the questions on the pro-poor policy in rural areas. How effective is the Act in addressing the problem of poverty among rural households? Are the poor able to get their rights? What are the limitations in the Act and its implementation?

The first chapter begins with an introduction on the concepts of public policy. It shows the importance of implementation studies in public policy. It also discusses about the research questions and the objectives of the research. A detail about the research methods employed in carrying out the research is also included.

The second chapter will look at the brief history of rural poverty alleviation programs in India since independence. It will also trace the progression of MGNREGA as a legal entitlement for guaranteed employment. This will give an idea on the significance of MGNREGA and how it is different from other poverty alleviation programs. The chapter will also deal with important provisions under MGNREGA and various other aspects. The chapter will look at the available studies on evaluation of MGNREGA.

The third chapter focuses on the state profile of Rajasthan. It endeavors to present the socio-economic profile of the state. It will analyse the functioning process of the administration in Rajasthan particularly in the context of implementing MGNREGA.

The fourth chapter will present the findings of the field survey carried out in the sample districts i.e. Dungarpur, Jhalawar, Sirohi and Udaipur. It will discuss the implementation of MGNREGA in the four districts. It will carry out a detailed analysis of the primary data collected from the field visit to the four districts.

The fifth chapter will draw a comparison on the implementation of MGNREGA in the four districts. It will look at the differences and similarity pattern in the implementation of MGNREGA in the four districts. It will try to look at the factors resulting in the differential pattern of implementation if any.

The sixth chapter will draw a conclusion with recommendations for further improvement in the implementation of the policy. It will also present an overview of the impact of the policy. Further, it will try to identify the factors responsible for the success as well as unsuccessful implementation of the policy.

MOITRI DEY

List of Tables

List of Figures/Pictures

ABBREVIATIONS

BDO	-	Block Development Officer
BPL	-	Below Poverty Line
CAG	-	Comptroller and Auditor General
CEGC	-	Central Employment Guarantee Council
CSRE	-	Crash Scheme for Rural Employment
DDP	-	Desert Development Programme
DPAP	-	Drought Prone Area Programme
DPC	-	District Programme Coordinator
DRSCs	-	Departmentally related Standing Committees
DRMU	-	Dakshini Rajasthan Mazdoor Union
DQM	-	District Quality Monitors
DWCRA	-	Development of Women and Children in Rural Areas
EAS	-	Employment Assurance Scheme
EGS	-	Employment Guarantee Scheme
FFWP	-	Food for Work Programme
GoI	-	Government of India
GP	-	Gram Panchayat
GS	-	Gram Sabha
GSDP	-	Gross State Domestic Product
HDI	-	Human Development Index
HDR	-	Human development Report
IAY	-	Indira Awas Yojana
ICDS	-	Integrated Child Development Scheme
IRDP	-	Integrated Rural Development Program
JC	-	Job Card
JGSY	-	Jawahar Gram Samridhi Yojana
JRY	-	Jawahar Rozgar Yojana
LPG	-	Liberalisation, Privatisation and Globalisation
MADA	-	Modified Area Development Approach
MFAL	-	Marginal Farmers and Agricultural Labourer

MGNREGA - Mahatma Gandhi National Rural Employment Guarantee Act
MIS - Management Information System
MKSS - Mazdoor Kisan Shakti Sanghatan
MoRD - Ministry of Rural Development
MWS - Million Wells Scheme
NAC - National Advisory Council
NGO - Non-Governmental Organisation
NQM - National Quality Monitors
NREGA - National Rural Employment Guarantee Act
NREGS - National Rural Employment Guarantee Scheme
NREP - National Rural Employment Programme
NSDP - Net State Domestic Product
NSSO - National Sample Survey Organisation
OBC - Other Backward Class
PEO - Programme Evaluation Organization
PIN - Professional Institutional Network
PIREP - Pilot Intensive Rural Employment Project
PMGY - Pradhan Mantri Gramodaya Yojana
PRI - Panchayati Raj Institution
REGS - Rural Employment Scheme
RLEGP - Rural Landless Employment Guarantee Programme
RREGS - Rajasthan Rural Employment Guarantee Scheme
RTI - Right to Information
SC - Scheduled Caste
SEGC - State Employment Guarantee Council
SFDA - Small Farmer Development Agency
SGRY - Sampoorna Grameen Rozgar Yojana
SGSY - Swarna Jayanti Gram Swarozgar Yojana
SHG - Self Help Group
SQM - State Quality Monitors
ST - Scheduled Tribe
TRYSEM - Training for Rural Youth for Self-Employment
UA - Unemployment Allowance
UNDP - United Nations Development Programme
UPA - United Progressive Alliance
VMC - Vigilance and Monitoring Committee
VMKS - Vagad Mazdoor Kisan Sanghathan
ZP - Zilla Parishad

1

Public Policy Implementation: A Concept

Public administration as an academic field of study is gaining utmost importance over the years. In India, which is on the path of rapid progress, the discourse of public administration is becoming significant. With increasing complexities of societies and diversified governmental activities, administration has a major role to play in society. Public administration with its interdisciplinary approach and policy orientation is an important area of study. According to Marini, "Public Administration can be defined in two ways i.e. as an occupation and as a field of study. As an occupation, public administration has to do with the formulation and implementation of policy of governmental and other public programs and the management of organizational activities involved. As an academic field of study it deals with the study, training and improvement of the above activities"[1]. Similarly, Dimock says that "Public administration is the fulfilment or enforcement of public policy as declared by the competent authority...Public administration is law in action. It is the executive side of the government".[2] L.D.White observes that "Public administration consists of all those operations having for their purpose the fulfilment or enforcement of public policy".[3] For Woodrow Wilson also public administration is detailed and systematic execution of public law.[4] The major activity of public administration is to make policies for the welfare of the public and implement it successfully. However, public administration still functions as the umbrella term throughout the world, though it must be realized that the term implies a broader range of concerns and activities than the narrow meaning of management or administration may convey.[5] Hanekom and Thornhill look at public administration as a concept that "consists of the functions of policy-making, organization, financing, staffing and the development of work procedure and control measures, which are performed in public institutions"[6]. It is important to clarify at this stage that there is a difference between Public Administration, written with capital letters and public administration, written with small letters. Public Administration refers to the subject or field of study and should be seen as the academic part. Public administration, written without capital letters refers to the phenomenon which is studied by the subject Public Administration and includes anything that can be observed in the public sector[7]. Therefore, Public Administration refers to a science whereas public administration refers to a practical phenomenon.

The science of public policy is management of policy planning, formation and its implementation by the government in common interest of the people. It is a branch of the wider field of public administration that deals with the machinery and procedure of policy formation in the public domain. Public policy formation is determined action taken in pursuit of a conscious purpose which facilitates systematic management of available resources to achieve a desired goal. Operating within a specific political setup, public policy envisages policy decisions of the political decision makers. The use of the world "public" in public policy restricts the area of its scope which refers to the study of policy formulation of the government (legislature, executive and judiciary). Therefore, public policy is the study of government's quest to formulate and implement various policies with special focus on the welfare of the people.

Understanding Public Policy

The 1950s saw the emergence of the study of public policy influenced by the policy sciences approach in America which later spread to Canada and Europe. The approach to the study of public policy was pioneered by Harold Lasswell who is known as the "Father of Policy Sciences". His essay, "The Policy Orientation" which is the opening chapter of H. Lasswell and Daniel Lerner's "The Policy Sciences" in 1957 heralded the studying of policy sciences[8]. Public Policy is studied as a part of Political Science, Public Administration, Economics and Management. However, with increasing demands of modern society, a need for more in-depth study of public policy was felt by the scholars of Political Science and Public Administration especially after the Second World War. Since then public policy is being studied as an independent discipline in various universities. The study of public policy has gone beyond the content of policy, processes of formulation and implementation. The concept of public policy is now in vogue particularly in the Third World countriens where rapid development is the agenda. With the increasing demands of the people, government is under constant pressure to answer these demand.

The policy sciences is an approach to understand and solve problems which can be local, regional or international. The policy sciences provide an integrated and comprehensive set of procedures for addressing them in ways that help to clarify and secure the common interest. The central objective of policy sciences is to help people make better decisions, and the fundamental goal is to foster a commonwealth of human dignity for all. Today, a growing number of people across academic disciplines, professions, and in civic life are finding that policy sciences offer a useful way to deal effectively with whatever problems they confront. In pursuit of this goal, the policy sciences draw on and contribute to all fields of knowledge.

In the words of H. Lasswell (1951)[9], policy sciences are concerned with the knowledge of and in the decision processes of the public and civil order. He focused on the rigorous application of science in the governance of a state. According to Harold Laswell policy sciences must stick to three principal attributes. First, is *contextuality*: decisions are part of a larger social process. The second is *problem orientation*: policy scientists are at home with the intellectual activities involved in clarifying goals, trends, conditions, projection, and alternatives. The third is *diversity*: the methods employed are not limited to a narrow range.

Yehezkel Dror uses the terms Megapolicy and Metapolicy as two facets of policy sciences. Megapolicy is the general direction or a blueprint or a framework of the future course of action of the government. It involves determination of the postures, assumption and main guidelines to be followed by specific policies. They are a kind of mega policy clearly distinct from detailed discrete policies[10]. Dror gave twelve main facets of mega policy viz, overall goals, policy boundaries, preference in time, risk acceptability, incrementalism versus innovation, comprehensiveness versus narrowness, balance oriented versus shock oriented, relevant assumptions on the future, theoretic basis, resource availability, range of policy instruments and pure versus mixed mega policy.

Metapolicy is the framework of policy formulation. Megapolicy is of limited use unless it is supplemented by the framework within which the specific policies would be formulated. Thus metapolicy and megapolicy are interdependent and together assist and improve policy analysis. Dror explains metapolicy as a "policy on how to make policy", and he firmly believes that unless this policy making system is reformed very little can be done to improve policies.

There is no denying to the fact that, the contributions of scholars of policy sciences have been enormous. However, there is a loose end in the studies of public policy which needs to be fastened according to the need of society. The approach of policy sciences have been American oriented for which the knowledge imparted by various scholars are not applicable in other countries particularly the developing countries. The credibility of policy sciences has justifiably been challenged for failing to produce objective empirical and normative truths. In the 1980s, the emphasis on ethics and values and the inclusion of institutional analysis and public management as central policy concerns improved the scope of the policy sciences but were ultimately injurious to the credibility of their scientific status[11]. The study of public policy gained importance with the approach of policy sciences.

Public policy is collective action taken by the political institutions for the welfare of its citizens. In other words, it is the result of the decisions of political institutions. It is a planned action of the government for the welfare of the public. Public policy is an action oriented and purposive decision taken by the government for a future course of action. It has been defined by various scholars working in the field of policy sciences. For better understanding of the concept, let us look at the various definitions of the scholars of public policy.

According to Thomas R. Dye (2004), "public policy is what the government chooses to do or not to do"[12].

To Sir Geoffrey Vickers (1983), "policies are decisions giving directions, coherence and continuity to the courses of action for which the decision-making body is responsible"[13].

James Anderson (1975) defines policy as a "purposive course of action or inaction undertaken by an actor or set of actors in dealing with a problem or matter of concern" [14].

Daneke and Steiss, (1978) says public policy is "A broad guide to present and future decisions, selected in light of given conditions from a number of alternatives; the actual decision or set of decisions designed to carry out the chosen course of actions; a projected program consisting of desired objectives (goals) and the means of achieving them.[15]"

According to Thomas A. Birkland (2005)[16], consensus is lacking on a more precise definition of public policy. Birkland outlines several possible definitions of public policy, always starting with the actions of government and the laws and appropriations that determine those actions. Birkland then indicates that the elements common to all definitions of public policy are: (1) It is made in the name of the "public"; (2) it is generally made or initiated by government; (3) it is interpreted and implemented by public and private players from corporations and non profit institutions; and (4) it also includes what the government chooses not to do.

Implementation Studies

Implementation is one of the important components in the policy making process. It is the active constituent of the process, thereby making it one of the most important pivots of policymaking. However, implementation study never received appropriate attention from the early scholars of policy studies. The study of policy implementation has a brief history. The approaches to study implementation started with the publication of Jeffrey Pressman and Aaron Wildavsky's influential book *"Implementation: How great expectations in Washington are dashed in Oakland?"* in 1973[17]. It was followed in 1975 by Erwin Hargrove's *"The Missing Link"* which emphasized the missing link that existed between policy making and the evaluation of the policy outcomes[18]. Towards the end of the twentieth, study of implementation started to expand and develop. The works explored the process of policy implementation and made a clear distinction between policy formulation and implementation (Derthick 1972[19], Pressman and Wildavsky 1973[20], Hargrove 1975[21], Berman 1978[22]). These works resulted in the debate of top-down and top-up approaches in the implementation study.

Policy Implementation is generally considered as a phase in the policy making process. It is a stage where a strategy is developed to organize the activities and personnel involved in the implementation process. The main task in implementation of a policy is of the administrative agencies or the bureaucrats. They organize and plan programmes and activities to be carried out step by step to bring the policy in effect. It has to manage the resources and funds available in a cost effective manner. The policy process also involves decision making at all the steps which is a crucial task for the administrative executives. The effectiveness of the policy to be implemented depends on the decision made by the implementing agencies. The implementation of a policy even after it is legitimized is not an easy task. The implementing agencies fill in the details so that it can be implemented successfully. It is a tedious and crucial exercise which needs to be carried out cautiously. It has been seen that in most of the third world countries the bureaucrats lack the capacity to carry out the activities of implementing policy. There is also lack of autonomy which restricts their decision making capacity. Hence, policy is implemented half heartedly and hardly serves the intended purpose.

The success of a policy is of immense importance to the government. In a democratic country like India, the successful implementation of a policy determines the stay of ruling government for a longer duration. With the increasing needs of the people, the government is now more inclined for successful implementation of policies. The study of implementation was neglected for many years. It has been seen that many studies were started to carry out in the 1970s to devise strategy for successful implementation of policies.

Implementation of a policy was a central concern but there was absence of literature. Implementation of policy was studied only as a part of policy process and focus was on the policy formulation. Policy formulation only provides the objectives of a goal. It doesn't provide any direction on how a policy is to be implemented to achieve the goal. As Mazmanian and Sabatier put it, "Knowing the (policy) objectives . . . (gives) only a general hint of what will actually be done by the agency responsible for carrying out the program and how successful it will be at winning the cooperation and compliance of the persons affected by it"[23]. Gunn (1978) argues, 'Academics have often seemed obsessed with policy formation while leaving the "practical details" of policy implementation to administrators'[24] (Smith and Larimer,2009[25]).

Goggin et al. (1990), traditionally divided the field of implementation studies into three generations. The story of implementation research across these generations starts with excitement over the possibility of breaking new intellectual ground, maturity and with it a more sober assessment of the intellectual challenges, to an ongoing debate over whether implementation studies are poised to move forward and fulfill their original promise or constitute an intellectual dead end and should be abandoned altogether[26].

The First Generation: The first generation of implementation studies comprises of the studies carried out initially in the 1970s. The first generation starts with the much acclaimed work of Jeffrey

Pressman and Aaron Wildavsky "Implementation: How Great Expectations in Washington Are Dashed in Oakland" in 1973[27]. Their main focus was the policy of Federal government to create 3000 jobs in inner-city Oakland. For them the policy was not the main interest but the failure of the government to achieve the policy objectives. Pressman and Wildavsky argued that the focus of their case study was, in effect, a best-case scenario for policy implementation. Another first generation scholar, Martha Derthick's examination of a federal program to build model communities on federally owned land in urban areas is also widely cited in the literature of implementation studies. The programme was intended to address a growing metropolitan crisis by building self-contained centrally planned "new towns" that would be socially and racially integrated. The programme was a failure and she highlighted the opposing perspectives at different governmental levels and lack of centralized coordination over implementation[28]. Both the studies show that the programmes failed due to lack of effective implementation. The studies call for understanding of cause and effect of implementation. This will help avoid repeats of the Oakland and new towns policy failures by laying out detailed steps for executing a particular policy or program, making democratic policymaking more effective.

The Second Generation: The first generation implementation studies were critically acclaimed for their limitations. The second generation implementation studies changed the trend of study into construction of implementation theory. The second generation implementation studies keeping in view the limitation of the first generation implementation studies started constructing framework of implementation process. The remarkable work started with Eugene Bardach's *The Implementation Game* in 1974. In his book, he classified implementation into a series of games. He also focused on the failure of policy like the first generation implementation studies and adds that, there are four basic "adverse effects" that can occur in the implementation process. They are: the diversion of resources, the deflection of policy goals, resistance to control and the dissipation of personal and political energy. He categorized his description of games according to each of these adverse effects. In short Bardach's theoretical framework saw implementation as an extension of politics but expanded the cast of actors[29].

Giandomenico Majone and Aaron Wildavsky, viewed implementation as shaped by general policy that is formally adopted but encompasses a wide range of goals, interactions, and dispositions, all of which are complexly connected. They did not consider the formal policy adoption as a set of marching orders. Instead, they saw agencies as the target population of policy and even policy makers as having to adapt to the goals and expectation created by policy[30].

Daniel Mazmanian and Paul Sabatier took a step further in their study on "Implementation and Public Policy", where they attempted to present empirically testable hypothesis on implementation[31]. They argued that there are three perspectives on the implementation of a policy. First, there is the perspective of what they term the "center" or the perspective of the initial policymaker. Implementation is a top-down trend and it is to achieve official policy objective. Second, it is the perspective of the "periphery" or the lower-level bureaucrats whose behavior actually translates the policy into action. It is all about how lower-level officials and institutions adapt to the shocks of their environment caused by higher-levels introducing new policies and programs. Thirdly, there is the perspective of the "target group" or the people at whom the policy is aimed at. It is about the impact the policies have on the lives of the targeted population. Mazmanian and Sabatier also recognized considerable overlap in these perspectives recognizing the difficulty in combining all three perspectives simultaneously into a single study or theory. Their theory is notable not just for being one of the first comprehensive theoretical frameworks of the implementation process, but because it highlights two critical issues that second generation implementation studies never fully resolved: perspective and complexity. It was, and is, not clear what perspective—center, periphery, target population, or some combination—provides the best starting point for building implementation theory.

Michael Lipsky is the name usually associated with the bottom-up approach and his notion of the street level bureaucrat created a powerful case[32]. He argued that Mazmanian and Sabatier's periphery was anything but peripheral when it came to determining what happened in implementation. To him the key actors in implementation are the people who actually did the implementing and the street level bureaucrats are the primary interface between citizens and government. The second generation implementation was marked by debates on top-down and bottom-up approaches in implementation studies.

The Third Generation: Malcolm Goggin and colleagues saw the end of 1980s as the third generation implementation studies when the focus was not only developing causal hypotheses but on rigorously testing them. The third generation tried to bridge the gap between the top-down and bottom-up approaches by incorporating both the approaches in their model of approach. They were also more scientific in their approach to the study of implementation[33]. Goggin et. al. further emphasized the aim of third generation studies, " to be more scientific than the previous two(generations) in its approach to the study of implementation. The third generation started off with a strong emphasis on scientifically testing the hypothesis of implementation. However, within a decade leading scholars (Lester and Goggin 1998[34]; de Leon 1999[35]; de Leon and de Leon 2002[36]) declared that only few studies have taken place and urged for its reconsideration.

The implementation studies have a brief history with varied contribution. The implementation studies started with a call by Pressman and Wildavsky. This was followed by various contributions to develop the theory of implementation. Various theories and studies were carried out in the early 1980s which developed a debate of top-down and bottom-up approaches to the study of implementation. After an endless debate on the two extreme approaches many scholars then tried to mix the two theories which came to be known as the synthesizer or the hybrid theory. The theories developed so far are limited to the implementation processes within the nation states rather than at the international level. Over the years many scholars are contributing substantially to the literature of implementation at the international level. There is a need for substantive research in implementation studies which can be applied in the different structures of different society.

Over the years many scholars are contributing substantially to the literature of implementation at the international level. There is a need for substantive research in implementation studies which can be applied in the different structures of diverse society.

Public Policy Implementation in India

According to Dye(2004), implementation involves all of the activities designed to carry out the policies enacted by the legislative branch. These activities include the creation of new organizations and departments, agencies, bureaus, and so on or the assignment of new responsibilities to existing organizations. These organizations must translate laws into operational rules and regulations. They must hire personnel, draw up contracts, spend money, and perform tasks. All of these activities involve decisions by bureaucrats and decisions that determine policy[37]. The government agencies at all levels of government are responsible for the implementation of policy which is important to understand. The implementation of a policy starts with organizing the implementation process. The implementation process involves a number of agencies/ actors who actively participate in each of the policy implementation course of action. The policies which have been finalized needs to be enforced and administered by organizing all the activities involved in an implementation process. This is generally carried out by the agencies authorized by the government. The roles and responsibilities of the agencies are specified by the government. The agencies involved in the implementation of policies in India are:

Administrative Agencies

The administrative agency is the permanent executive who looks after the government's day to day work. The institution of bureaucracy is the main administrative agency for implementing public policy in India. The pivotal role of bureaucracy in the implementation of public policy has been widely acknowledged by the scholars of policy studies. Bureaucracy has a major role to play in interpreting legislation and putting into effect the regulations and implementing laws and policies. Bureaucracy is a hierarchical institution comprising of professionalized, trained and expert officials. The Indian bureaucracy is an enormously complex system which consists of the All India Services, State Services, employees of the local governments, and technical and managerial staff running public sector undertakings. In a democracy like India there is possibility of defeating the ruling party in the elections which means that a new government might take up new policies in place of the previous policies of the government. The bureaucrats are expected to be politically neutral and do not take any political position on policy matters.

The role of administrative agency is vital in policy making. Their role is to help the political executive in identifying the problems, searching for the alternatives in the process of formulation of a policy and finally handle its implementation. It is often said that policy making is the work of the political executive and it is the permanent executive i.e. bureaucracy which is responsible for implementing the policy. The role of bureaucracy is not only confined to the implementation of policy but pervades the entire policy making process. The political executive is to a large extent dependent on the bureaucracy for policy making and its implementation. The bureaucratic administration breaks the absolute power of elected leadership or monarchy due to its systematized administration. The bureaucracy is expected to practice autonomy and independence in giving its opinion to political leaders and faithfully execute the policy.

The legislature and the political executive cannot cope with the increasing functions of the legislature as well as the activities in their own constituency. It has been generally seen that the political executive takes more interest in the policy making and delegate the policy for implementation to the bureaucracy. The political executive delegates most of its work to the bureaucracy for filling the details after a broad framework of policy is made. Thus it is the responsibility of the bureaucracy to analyze the policy proposals in relation to the provisions of the Constitution, the laws framed by the Parliament and other existing rules and regulations. The bureaucracy is the repository of information about the past policies and programmes and has all the relevant information and data required for the implementation of policies. With the inputs of relevant data, the bureaucracy plans the execution of the policies in an efficient manner keeping in view the objectives of the policy and limited resources available. One of their main tasks is financial planning. The programmes under the policies are carried out in accordance with the financial availability. The available budget has to be dispersed equally for the activities involved in the policy implementation process. They are also accountable to the legislature for financial allocation. The legislature in turn is accountable to the citizen. The bureaucracy has trained expertise in their profession which help them to implement the policies in an effective and innovative way. They make rules and regulation to carry out the activities of the policies to be carried out. They plan and organize the available personnel with specific role and responsibility. It is also their duty to keep a check on the progress of the work. In this sense they act as a regulator of the activities. They also monitor and constantly provide feedback of the policies being implemented.

The bureaucracy plays a vital role in delivering the welfare policies of the government to the people. The bureaucracy has been given enormous power by the legislature to carry out the implementation of policies. However, it has often been seen that the ever increasing power of bureaucracy and over-dependency of political executive on bureaucracy has a negative impact on the people. It has been observed that the bureaucracy is becoming insensitive to the demands and expectations of the ordinary citizen. The representatives of the people in the government need to control and keep a track of their activities carried out in the implementation of the policies. But there is also a fear that too much political interference may turn the bureaucracy into an instrument in the hands of the politician. There is also lack of enough provisions for accountability of the bureaucracy to the citizen. It is expected that measures like Right to Information may make the bureaucracy a little more responsive and accountable. However, the bureaucracy needs to be committed to the welfare of the people only then it can implement public policies effectively.

Legislative Agencies

The Constituent Assembly of India opted for a parliamentary system of Government in India. Parliamentary democracy is a form of governance where people rule through their representatives in Parliament chosen by adult suffrage through free and fair elections. The Parliament consists of the President and the two Houses i.e. *Lok Sabha* (Lower House) and *Rajya Sabha* (Upper House). The *Lok Sabha* or the House of the people is composed of representatives elected by the people through direct election under universal adult suffrage. There are 545 members, out which two are appointed by the President from the Anglo-Indian community if it is not represented adequately.

The *Rajya Sabha* or Council of States is composed of representatives of each state elected by the Legislative Assembly of the State in accordance with the system of proportional representation by means of the single transferable vote. The *Rajya Sabha* has 250 members out of which 12 members are nominated by the President from among persons having "special knowledge or practical experience in literature, science, art and social service. The policies in India are initiated, debated and passed by the Parliament to make it a law. The role of Parliament is not confined to the policy making process only but also to the effective implementation of policies.

As has been discussed earlier due to the prominent role of bureaucracy and the Cabinet the significance of Parliament has gradually declined. Since Parliament has paucity of time, its role in implementation of policy is diminishing but it has a crucial role to play in the functioning of the administration. They have to check the work done by the administrators so that they function efficiently. To keep an eye on the functioning of the bureaucracy the Parliament has a number of Committees which keep a track on the activities of the bureaucracy. The committees are on Subordinate Legislation, the Committee on Government Assurances, the Committee on Estimates, the Committee on Public Accounts and the Committee on Public Undertakings and Departmentally related Standing Committees (DRSCs). The Committee on Estimates, the Committee on Public Accounts, the Committee on Public Undertakings and DRSCs play an important role in exercising a check over governmental expenditure and policy formulation and implementation.

The Committees appointed by the Parliament can indirectly control the functioning of the bureaucracy. It can keep an eye on the efficiency of the bureaucracy and also influence the actions of the bureaucracy. There are also specific Committees of particular sections of the society like the Committee on the Welfare of Scheduled Castes and Scheduled Tribes and Committee on Empowerment of Women. They also influence the policies related to the welfare of particular sections (like Scheduled Castes, Scheduled Tribes or Women) and coerce on the effective implementation of the policies.

Judicial Agency

In India under the Constitution a single integrated system of courts for administering both the Union and State laws has been adopted. The Judiciary is an independent body and separate from the Executive and Legislative bodies. The Supreme Court of India is at the head of the entire system which is followed by the High Courts at the state level, District courts at the district level and *Lok Adalat* at the village and *panchayat* level. The Chief Justice of India and 25 other judges constitute the Supreme Court. All the judges in the Supreme Court of India are appointed by the President of India. The Supreme Court of India acts as the guardian of the Constitution and the law declared by it is binding on all other courts within the territory of India. It ensures that the rights of the citizens are not trespassed by the government.

The Judiciary is an important agency which ensures that the rights of the citizens are not surpassed by the government and also the government works within the powers conferred by the Constitution. The Supreme Court and the high courts have been empowered to exercise judicial review of the legislation. Judicial review is nowhere mentioned in the Constitution but the fact that India has a written Constitution and the power of the Supreme Court to strike down a law that goes against the fundamental rights of the citizens gives the Supreme Court the power of judicial review. Judicial power can influence on the effective implementation of policy. It can also nullify or stop the implementation of a particular policy through their interpretations of statutes and executive decisions. The Judiciary clarifies the provisions of the policy in case those are vague and susceptible to different interpretation. The Judiciary can pass judgments on actions taken during the implementation encroaching on the rights of the citizen or against the Constitutional provisions.

In short, the Supreme Court which is the apex body in the judicial system of India acts as the guardian of the Constitution.

Panchayati Raj Institutions

Part IV of the Constitution of India, Article 40 of the Indian Constitution states that the state shall take steps to organize village *panchayat* and endow them with such powers and authority as may be necessary to enable them to function as units of self government. Local governance is one of the ways to bring about democracy at the grass roots level which has been one the main objectives of democratic India. It is not only a convenient administrative setup but also a platform for the people to participate in the democracy of the country and gives an opportunity for self governance which ensures the consent of the people in the decision making process of the country. The 73rd Constitutional Amendment Act, 1992 which is a landmark in the history of PRI gives a uniform status to the institution of *panchayati raj* in the whole country. It provides for a three tier *panchayati raj* system for a state exceeding the population of 20 lakhs. Specifically, it empowers states to endow *panchayat* with such powers and authority as to enable them to function as institutions of self-government (Article 243-G of the Constitution). Since the Constitutional amendment all the rural development programmes have been mandated to involve PRIs in its implementation.

In India, *panchayati raj* institution (PRI) has a significant role to play in the implementation of government policies at the grassroot level. To enhance the democratic process and bring about changes in the lives of the people at the grassroot level, the government has empowered the PRI with planning, monitoring and implementation of rural programmes. One of the main functions of PRI is to implement schemes and policies for economic development and social justice as may be entrusted to them including those in relation to the matters listed in the Eleventh Schedule. These subjects are related to functions linked to the welfare of the local people.

The *panchayat* conduct *gram sabha*[38] in the villages and disseminate information of all the government policies and programs. They also spread information through hoardings, posters, street plays, etc. PRI is an important medium of the government to spread awareness among the rural population who are mostly illiterate. During the *gram sabha,* the planning of implementing the policies is discussed and decisions for the same are taken. They also conduct surveys in the villages to identify the targeted population for implementing the policies taken up by the government. Since they have a fair knowledge of the local conditions, it is easier for the PRI to execute the policies or programmes of the government accordingly. This leaves least scope for the policy to be unsuccessful.

The PRI prepares the plan document for executing policies and gets it approved from the higher authority. The PRI executes the works as planned and decided in the *gram sabha*. They also maintain the records of the policies being implemented. The PRI decides the financial allocation as per the sanctioned budget and keeps an account of the financial spending. Monitoring and supervising the execution of policies is also the duty of the PRI.

Social auditing of government policies is in vogue now. The PRI conducts social auditing of the government policies and report to the government on the performance of the policies. It provides a feedback to the government for further rectification of the policies and delivery mechanisms. The PRI listens to the grievances and complaints of the rural people regarding the policies and try to address their grievances. The villagers also have a tendency of not sharing their problems with higher officials who are like strangers to them and are at ease with people at the *panchayat* level who are mostly people from their locality. However it has been often found that the PRI are not given enough autonomy to carry out their functions smoothly. This creates a hindrance in the execution of polices and PRI becomes less enthusiastic about the development policies. They also suffer from lack of administrative and technical support while carrying out their functions. Most of the people in the PRI lack capacity and are not provided enough training by the government. They are unable to handle critical situations in the execution process. The government needs to provide sufficient support to strengthen the PRI for successful implementation of the policies.

Civil Society

Civil society is one of those people centered; micro-level organizations that work for the people and are expected to encourage people to participate in the development process in an effective manner. It is also often called the third tier of the government other than the state and the market. Civil society consists of non-governmental organizations (NGOs), registered trusts, trade unions, community groups, women's organizations, religious organizations, etc. Some of these organizations work for profit but most of them are non-profit voluntary organizations. These organizations are diverse in terms of structure, objectives, operation mechanism, and target groups. Despite this diversity one commonality is that, most of these organizations deal with common concerns of people and issues of societal development, social upliftment of marginalized groups. The major activity of such organization is to ensure the needs of disadvantaged groups excluded from mainstream development. The role of civil society organizations has become important which can not only provide support to government but also can encourage people to participate in different ways for making government programmes successful.

In India the socio-economic policies for the development of the marginalized sections of the society have not reached the targeted populations. Despite investment for decades the policies are not effective in curbing the socio-economic problems. It has been seen that the delivery system of the policy is not competent enough to serve the purpose. In view of this failure of government to successfully implement the policies, many voluntary and non government organizations which are also called civil society organizations have come forward to share the burden of government in the process of policy implementation. NGO is a legally constituted organization and operates independently from any government with some objective of attaining social goals like improvement of literacy status, sustainable livelihood, environment protection, women empowerment and so on. In India, many policy interventions have been undertaken and several schemes have been introduced after Independence for rapid development but often these schemes and resources have bypassed poor and disadvantaged people who needed these most. The funds have been usurped by the non-poor with their vested interest of exploiting the poor. The poverty reduction programme could not reduce poverty and in fact, the benefits meant for poor were preempted by the non-poor. It is because of this, it was felt that people should be empowered to participate in government programmes that are introduced for their benefit. Their participation was needed from the beginning and was expected to be continued at every stage of implementation of policies. It was required to develop awareness of people and to develop their capacity by providing information, knowledge and skills to participate in decision making process which has been acknowledged as the basic requirement for developing a vibrant democratic society and its substance. According to Rajasekhar, "The need for micro-level institutional arrangement to involve the people in formulation, implementation and monitoring of the programmes, is therefore, stressed in several quarters."[39]

For the last two-three decades NGOs have started playing a prominent role in the implementation of public policies. They spread awareness, acceptance and knowledge to the people about the policies of the government. They also lobby for a particular social cause and carry out activities for the cause. The government under their pressure comes out with innovative policies. The recent right based polices like the Right to Information, the Mahatma Gandhi National Rural Guarantee Act, the Right to Education and Right to Food are all influenced by many NGOs. They reach the people at the grassroot level and spread the messages of the policies and act as a link between the government and the people. They also keep a strict vigil on the implementation of government policies. They carry out studies to see the progress and problem of the policies being implemented. In this sense, they also serve as the eyes and ears of the people.

The pressure groups on the other hand influence the policy implementation process in an opportunistic manner. They use any method or technique which they believe will serve their purpose. Keeping in view their interest they influence the policy implementers to get the policy implemented in the manner whereby the pressure groups reap maximum benefits. It can use its influence either in helping the successful execution of the policy or standing in the way of the implementation depending on their interest. They use the method of lobbying, strikes, carrying out rally, etc to pressurize the government for executing policies in their interest. The pressure group has the organizational capacities to help the implementing agencies in the implementation of any policy. In India it has been seen that the role of pressure groups with regard to implementation of policy is parochial. These pressure groups can be of enormous use to the society at large if they try to make use of the mobilized public opinion in a more positive manner. It is worth mentioning that the role of civil society lies in supplementing the efforts of the government and not in competition with the government.

Policy implementation involves multiple actors as discussed above. Each actor has a specific role to play in the implementation process. In practice it has been seen that most of the actors involved in the implementation process are not able to perform their assigned role. It has been seen that there is lack of clear defined roles and responsibility of the stakeholders which creates differences among the stake holders. This often leads to poor implementation of the policies and sometimes a failure of policy. Wu et.al (2010) pointed that "policy makers often fail to prepare the ground systematically for implementation, resulting occasionally in high-profile policy disasters and even more frequently in policies that perform far below expectation"[40]. Similarly Pressman and Wildavsky in their famous book also stressed on the gap between the policy formulated and implemented[41].

The reality is quite different then what has been predicted by the policy makers. Policies which are not implemented as designed then the outcome of the policies will be sad. The policy which does not serve the targeted population is considered to be a poor or ineffective policy. It is also known as a failed policy. In practice it has been observed that sound implementation of policy is the most challenging task in the policy making process. The policy formulators do not have a clear picture of reality at the ground level and the needs of the targeted population which ultimately result in ineffective implementation of policies. Before a policy is implemented, a favorable condition needs to be prepared so that a policy can be implemented without any hindrance.

The problems in policy implementation are more prominent in the Third World countries. Since most of the Third World countries lack infrastructure, finance, expert personnel, etc. a policy might not be as effective as those implemented in Western countries. Generally the policies in Western countries are incremental in nature. The concern of the policies remains the same with little changes in the policy design. However, Third World countries have just started with the development process with their limited resources which leaves less scope for incremental policies. It is also widely accepted that incremental policies are easier to implement than ambitious non-incremental policies. Western countries face policy failures in case of non- incremental policies[42].

Similarly in India, there is a lack of proper implementation of public policies. There is no systematic detailed analysis of policy before it is made and implemented. It has been pointed out by Mathur and Mathur that due to India's post colonial developing country orientation, policymaking and policy research have been framed through the terms of "development" and "planning"[43]. They found that while a well developed field of policy analysis has yet to be clearly identified, public administration as a subject of study and an applied field has received most attention in India. Currently, there is a strong trend in the growth of the activity of documentation of the institutional bases of policy analysis and research capacity; however a reflection on tools and methodologies of analysis has yet to be emerged as an important theme in mainstream academia.

From the above discussion, we can say that implementation of a policy is of utmost importance. It has also been seen that there is a gap between policy formation and its expected outcome i.e. its implementation. Implementation studies as we have discussed, have a short history which means that there is lack of extensive study of implementation of policies. Moreover, the implementation studies carried so far are West-oriented which leaves less scope for its applicability in other countries particularly in the developing and under-developing countries. A successful implementation of a programme depends on a strong, well defined and systematically analysed policy.

In India, it is the Planning Commission which works as core policy institution and plans for the socio-economic development of the country. So planning and policy making are treated equally. There is no proper policy analysis done when policy decisions are made. This ultimately leads to a faulty policy design and unsuccessful policy implementation. There is a need of a separate body comprising of experts in policy analysis to carry out policy studies in India.

Based on the above context, the book will look at the Implementation of Mahatma Gandhi National Rural Employment Guarantee Act (MGNREGA) in Rajasthan.

The Indian Government passed the Mahatma Gandhi National Rural Employment Guarantee Act (MGNREGA) in September, 2005 and launched the National Rural Employment Guarantee Programme on February 2, 2006. The Act guarantees the right to work by providing 100 days of guaranteed wage employment in a financial year to every rural household whose adult members are willing to do unskilled manual work. MGNREGA is the first ever law internationally, that guarantees wage employment at an unprecedented scale. The idea is to give a legal guarantee of employment to anyone who is willing to do casual manual labour at the statutory minimum wage. Any adult who applies for work under the Act is entitled to being employed on public works without delay. Thus, an Employment Guarantee Act provides a universal and enforceable legal right to the most basic form of employment. The enactment of the Act was a major achievement for Indian democracy. However, the real essence of the Act lies in its successful implementation of the Act. The book intends to answer some of the questions on the pro-poor policy in rural areas. How effective is the Act in addressing the problem of poverty among rural households? Are the poor able to get their rights? What are the limitations in the Act and its implementation?

In view of these, a focused study was carried out in Rajasthan. Rajasthan was selected because of its pioneering role in the enactment and implementation of the Act. The origin for enactment of the Act can also be traced back to Rajasthan. The people's movement in Rajasthan led to the enactment of Right to Information Act (RTI) and MGNREGA. The people of Rajasthan were actively engaged in the long struggle for RTI, MGNREGA and the current right to food campaign spearheaded by civil society organizations particularly the Mazdoor Kisan Shakti Sangathan(MKSS). This created awareness about the MGNREGA to the people before it was enacted. In the initial phase of implementation of MGNREGA, positive impacts have been seen in Rajasthan. Rajasthan also has a history of positive achievements of other rural development programs of Government of India. Rajasthan is a dry region where MGNREGA can be a fortunate thing to restore the till now marginalized rural economy.

Research Methodology

To explore all the aspects of implementing a policy, the study employs triangulation method. In social science triangulation is defined as the mixing of data or methods so that diverse viewpoints or standpoints cast light upon a topic. [44]Triangulation refers to the use of more than one approach to the investigation of a research question in order to enhance confidence in the ensuing findings. Since much social research is founded on the use of a single research method and as such may suffer from limitations associated with that method or from the specific application of it, triangulation offers the prospect of enhanced confidence. Webb et al. stressed that, "Once a proposition has been confirmed by two or more independent measurement processes, the uncertainty of its interpretation is greatly reduced. The most persuasive evidence comes through a triangulation of measurement processes"[45]. Denzin says that "Since each method has restrictions, by combining several methods in the same study the restrictions of one tool are often the strengths of another[46]. The study is an evaluation study based on both qualitative and quantitative method. Using triangulation method helps to discover the links between various dimensions of implementing a policy.

Qualitative research describes reality as experienced by the groups, communities, individuals, etc[47]. It provides information about the human side of an issue i.e. the often contradictory behaviors, beliefs, opinions, emotions, and relationships of individuals. Qualitative methods are also effective in identifying intangible factors, such as social norms, socioeconomic status, gender roles, ethnicity and religion. When used along with quantitative methods, qualitative research can help us to interpret and better understand the complex reality of a given situation and the implications of quantitative data. The impact of MGNREGA on lives of rural poor and various social dimensions can be identified. It can explore the socioeconomic changes of the beneficiaries of MGNREGA in the study area.

Quantitative methods refer to quantitative measurement by using survey methods, questionnaire, interviews, etc. It helps to predict, explain and understand the causal relationships of some phenomenon. The greatest strength of quantitative research is that it produces quantifiable, reliable data that are usually generalizable to some larger population. It is important to note that qualitative-quantitative dichotomy in research methods is not very accurate: what is quantitative is not necessarily qualitative and vice versa[48]. This method can identify the gaps and reason in the implementation of MGNREGA. It can be the basis for indepth analysis of the successful implementation of the Act in a particular sampled area.

Research Tools

The study started with reviewing secondary data in the initial phase. Various literatures on public policy, poverty policies and rural development which consist of books, research articles, policy briefs and internet sources were reviewed. This gave an insight on the concepts of public policy making and implementation policy. This helped in identifying the significance of implementation study in public policy process. On the basis of these concepts, a wide range of reports provided by government agencies, institutions, think-tanks, articles and newspaper reports on the implementation of MGNREGA have been reviewed thoroughly.

The primary source of data is based on the survey conducted in the study area. After an assessment of the available literature on MGNREGA and the operation guidelines on MGNREGA provided by the Ministry of Rural Development, Government of India, the following parameters were used to develop the questionnaires for beneficiaries and *Panchayat* members.

- Socio-economic profile
- Awareness
- Participation
- On-Demand Job Duration
- Payment Details
- Worksite Facilities
- Transparency
- Monitoring and Supervision
- Overall Impact

A semi-structured questionnaire was also developed for

interviewing the officials involved in the implementation of MGNREGA. The questionnaires and schedule are provided at the end of the book as Appendix.

Observation implies the use of eyes rather than ears and voice. It is watching and noting of phenomena as they occur with regard to the cause and effect or mutual relations[49]. The observation at the worksites while conducting interviews revealed the impact on the lives of the rural people. During visits to the villages, as a participant observer and interaction with the villagers helped in identifying some of the loopholes in the implementation of the Act. In depth observations was done with regard to the functioning of *Panchayati Raj Institution* (PRI) and their role in the implementation of the Act. The perspectives of community members, PRI members and officials were also taken into consideration on issues pertinent to implementing the Act.

Sampling

A sample is a part of the larger population. It represents the entire population and enables the researcher to deal with a smaller number of persons. It ensures that there is accuracy in the detailed study and helps in generalizing the outcomes. Manheim says that "a sample is a part of the population which is studied in order to make inferences about the whole population"[50]. Sampling is the knowledge we seek about the total population called the universe by observing a few units called sample and extend our inference about the sample to the entire population[51].

Universe of the Study

The study has taken up Rajasthan as a case study. Four districts of Rajasthan Dungarpur, Jhalawar, Sirohi and Udaipur were selected for a comparison on the impact analysis of the Act. A comparative strategy can help in identifying the drawbacks and advantages in the implementation of the Act. It provides a better understanding of constraints pertaining to institutions and the environment.

Sampling Frame

Sampling frame refers to the basis on which the samples representing the universe are selected. The Act was implemented in a phase manner with a total of 200 districts in the first phase on February, 2006. In 2007-08, the same was extended to 130 additional districts and by 1st April, 2008, the remaining districts of India were covered with the exception of districts that have a hundred percent urban population. MGNREGA was implemented in the initial phase in the four districts, Dungarpur, Jhalawar, Sirohi and Udaipur.

In each district two blocks were selected using purposive sampling technique. Smith defined this as a sampling that rests on the assumption that knowledge is unequally distributed and that different participants provide a series of general, specific and marginal observations[52]. The assumption behind purposive sampling is that by using good judgement and an appropriate strategy, the researcher, can handpick the cases to be included and develop samples that are satisfactory. By using this technique the researcher can use her expertise to select subjects who represent the population being studied[53]. In a purposive sample, respondents are chosen because they possess the necessary characteristics and they are accessible to the researcher. Since MGNREGA is implemented at the *gram panchayat* level two *gram panchayats*, one in each block was selected using snowball technique. This is a type of non-probability sampling method used when it is difficult to approach the target population. This technique was employed as the sample area was totally new for the researcher. In each of the *gram panchayat*, 30 respondents who benefitted from the Act were interviewed. The interview of the beneficiaries was conducted in the ongoing worksite if any or in the villages. The detail of the sample is provided in the following Table I.

Table 1.1: Details of the Sample

Districts	Blocks	Gram Panchayat	No. of Beneficiaries Interviewed
Dungarpur	Asspur	Gol	30
	Bicchiwada	Bicchiwada	30
Total			60
Jhalawar	Jhalrapatan	Durgpura	30
	Pirawa	Sunel	30
Total			60
Sirohi	Abu Road	Kivli	30
	Pindwara	Jhadoli	30
Total			60
Udaipur	Gogunda	Gogunda	30
	Salumber	Amlodha	30
Total			60
Overall Total			240

In addition, interview with selected Panchayat functionaries identified through purposive sampling was conducted. They were interviewed for their opinion to assess the demand for job and issues related to the access to job. The Block Development Officers (B.D.O.) in each block was also interviewed using open ended questionnaires to get further insights on the implementation of the Act.

Endnotes

1 Frank Marini(2000) "Public Administration" in M.Shafritz edited *Defining Public Administration: Selections from the International Encyclopedia of Public Policy and Administration*; Westview Press, USA p.3

2 Dimock E. Marshall (1937) "The Study of Administration"; American Political Science Review, Feb 1937,pp.31-32.

3 L.D.White (1955) "Introduction to the Study of Public Administration"; Macmillan Co., New York. P.1

4 Woodrow Wilson (1887) "The Study of Administration";Political Science Quarterly;Vol.2.No.2 ,June.pp.197-222

5 Frank Marini (2000) "Public Administration" in M.Shafritz (ed.) *Defining Public Administration: Selections from the International Encyclopedia of Public Policy and Administration*; Westview Press, USA p.4

6 S.X. Hanekom,& C.Thornhill (1993) "Public Administration in Contemporary Society: A South African Perspective"; Revised edition. Southern, Pretoria p.9

7 P.Harris(1990) "Foundation of public administration: A Comparative Approach"; University Press, Hong Kong p.74

8 H.D. Lasswell(1951) "The Policy Orientation" in D.Lerner and H.D.Lasswell(ed.) *The Policy Sciences*; Stanford University Press, Palo Alto, California.

9 *Ibid.*

10 Yehezkel Dror(1971) "Design for Policy Sciences" American Elsevier,New York. p. 53.

11 Peter de Leon and Vogenbeck M. Danielle (2007a) "Back to Square One: The History and Promise of the Policy Sciences" in Jack Rabin,et.al (3rd ed.), *Handbook of Public Policy Administration*, CRC Press, Taylor and Francis Group, Florida pg.504

12 Thomas Dye (2004) "Understanding Public Policy"; (10th ed.) Pearson, New Delhi.

13 Sir Geoffrey Vickers (1983) "The Art of Judgment"; (2nd ed.) Chapman and Hall, London.

14 James E Anderson (1975) "Public Policy Making"; Praeger, New York

15 Gregory A. Daneke and Alan Walter Steiss(1978) "Planning and Policy Analysis for Public Administrators" in John W. Sutherland (ed.), *Management Handbook for Public Administrators*, Van Nostrand and Reinhold Company, New York.

16 Thomas A Birkland (2005) "An Introduction to the Policy Process: Theories,

Concepts and Models of Public Policy Making" ;(2nd ed.) Armonk, M.E. Sharpe, New York

17 Jeffrey Pressman and Aaron Wildavsky (1973) "Implementation: How Great Expectations in Washington Are Dashed in Oakland"; University of California Press, Berkeley.

18 Erwin C. Hargrove (1975) "The Missing Link: The Study of the Implementation of Social Policy"; Urban Institute, Washington, DC.

19 Martha Derthick (1972) "New Towns In-Town: Why a Federal Program Failed"; The Urban Institute, Washington, DC

20 *Ibid.*

21 *Ibid.*

22 P. Berman(1978) "The Study of Macro and Micro Implementation"; Public Policy; 26(2):157-84

23 D.A. Mazmanian and P.A. Sabatier (1983) "Implementation and Public Policy"; Glenview, Ill.: Scott, Foresman.pp. 4-5

24 L.Gunn (1978) 'Why is implementation so difficult?';Management Services in Government, 33 (4): 169–76.

25 Kevin B. Smith and Christopher W.Larimer,(2009) " The Public Policy Theory Primer"; Westview Press, Central Avenue, Boulder, CO 80301

26 Malcolm Goggin, Ann O'M. Bowman, James Lester, and Laurence O'Toole Jr. (1990) "Implementation Theory and Practice: Towards a Third Generation"; Foresman Scott / Brown Little Glenview, Illinios.

27 *Ibid.*

28 *Ibid.*

29 Eugene Bardach (1974) "The Implementation Game: What Happens After a Bill Becomes Law"; MIT Press, Cambridge, MA.p.64

30 Giandomenico Majone and Aaron Wildavsky (1978) "Implementation as Evolution" in H. Freeman (ed.) *Policy Studies ReviewAnnual*; Sage, Beverly Hills. pp. 103–117

31 *Ibid.*, pp. 12-13.

32 *Ibid.*, pp. 18 & 462.

33 Malcolm Goggin, Ann O'M. Bowman, James Lester, and Laurence O'Toole Jr. (1990) "Implementation Theory and Practice: Towards a Third Generation"; Glenview, IL: Scott, Foresman/Little, Brown.pp.18 & 462

34 James Lester and Malcolm Goggin (1998) "Back to the Future: The Rediscovery of Implementation Studies"; Policy Currents, September: 1–7.

35 Peter de Leon (1999) "The Missing Link Revisited: Contemporary Implementation Research"; Policy Studies Review 16: 311–339.

36 Peter de Leon and Linda de Leon (2002) "What Ever Happened to Policy Implementation? An Alternative Approach"; Journal of Public Administration Research and Theory 12: 467–492.

37 Thomas Dye (2004) "Understanding Public Policy" ;(10th ed.) Pearson, New Delhi.pp.52

38 A *gram sabha* is a body of all persons entered as electors in the electoral roll for a *gram panchayat*. All the meetings of the *gram sabha* are convened by the *gram panchayat* to disseminate information to the people as well as to ensure that development of the village is done through participation or consent of all households.

39 D. Rajasekhar (1999) "Decentralized Government and NGOs"; Concept Publication, New Delhi. p.2.

40 Xun Wu, M.Ramesh, Michael Howlett and Scott Fritzen(2010), "The Public Policy Primer: Managing the Policy Process" Routledge, New York

41 Jeffrey L. Pressman and Aaron Wildavsky(1973) "Implementation: How great expectations in Washington are Dashed in Oakland" University of California Press, Berkeley, CA.

42 Thomas B Smith (1973) "The Policy Implementation Process"; Policy Sciences; Vol.4, No.2; pp 197-209.

43 Navdeep Mathur and Kuldeep Mathur(2006) "Policy Analysis in India:Research Bases and Discursive Practices" in Frank Fischer, Gerald J.Miller and Marn S.Sidney (ed.) *Handbook of Public Policy Analysis:Theory Politics and Methods*; CRC Press, Florida, USA.p.603

44 Wendy Oslen(2004) "Triangulation in Social Research: Qualitative and Quantitative Methods Can Really Be Mixed" in M. Holborn (ed.) *Development in Sociology* ; Causeway Press, Oranskisk

45 E. J Webb, D. T. Campbell, R. D.Schwartz and L.Sechrest, (1966) "Unobtrusive Measures: Nonreactive Measures in the Social Sciences" Rand McNally, Chicago. p.3.

46 N.K. Denzin(1970) "The Research Act in Sociology";Aldine, Chicago.

47 Ram Ahuja (2005) "Research Methods"; Rawat Publications, Jaipur.

48 Vatche Gabrielian (1999) "Qualitative Research Method: An Overview" in Gerald J.Miller and Marcia L. Whicker (ed.) *Handbook of Research Method in Public Administration;* Marcel Dekker, New York

49 *Ibid.*

50 Henry L.Manheim(1977) "Sociological Research: Philosophy & Methods"; The Dorsey Press,Illinois.p.270

51 *Ibid.*, pp. 159.

52 M. Smith (1988) "Strategies and Social Research"; Prentice Hall, Englewood Cliffs. p.118

53 L. Bailey (1982) "Methods of Social Research."; The Free Press, New York.p.100

2

Mahatma Gandhi National Rural Employment Guarantee Act: An Introduction

Poverty has been one of the major concerns of independent India. India remains predominantly a rural nation, with 68.8 percent[1] of its people living in rural areas. Different reports also reveal high incidence of rural poverty for example, the number of poor people in India according to the country's Eleventh National Development Plan, amounts to more than 300 million[2].In the 1990s, India underwent economic reforms which made India, the fourth largest economy in the world. However, this economic development has not been equally beneficial to the people in the country. Those who are left behind are still lagging behind while those who have benefitted are prospering. The Mahatma Gandhi National Rural Employment Guarantee Act (MGNREGA) is a milestone in India's rural poverty alleviation programs. The Government of India passed the Mahatma Gandhi National Rural Employment Guarantee Act in September, 2005 and launched the National Rural Employment Guarantee Programme on February 2, 2006. The Act guarantees right to work by providing 100 days of guaranteed wage employment in a financial year to every rural household whose adult members are willing to do unskilled manual work. MGNREGA is the first ever law internationally, that guarantees wage employment at an unprecedented scale. The idea is to give a legal guarantee of employment to anyone who is willing to do casual manual labour at the statutory minimum wage. Any adult who applies for work under the Act is entitled to being employed on public works without delay. Thus, an employment guarantee Act provides a universal and enforceable legal right to the most basic form of employment. It is a step towards legal enforcement of the right to work, as an aspect of the fundamental right to live with dignity[3]. It was implemented in 200 districts in the first phase and the same was extended to 130 additional districts in 2007-2008. The remaining districts of the country have been covered under the MGNREGA with effect from April 1,2008. Thus, MGNREGA covers the entire country with the exception of districts that have a hundred percent urban population.

According to the Act, the State Government is directed to prepare a Rural Employment Scheme (REGS) within six months in order to implement the work guarantee. Thus, the Act provides the legal foundation of work guarantee, and the Scheme is the means through which this guarantee comes into effect. Although each state is free to frame its own Rural Employment Guarantee Scheme, this is subject to certain "basic features" that are spelt out in Schedule I of the Act. Each REGS is also supposed to follow the "Operational Guidelines" issued by the Ministry of Rural Development in January 2006. However, it is not mandatory for the states to follow the operational guideline which results in half hearted implementation of the Act. It is one of the major programmes launched by the United Progressive Alliance (UPA) government in India to address the issue of rural poverty. It is a step forward from previous poverty alleviation programmes because the previous programmes did not put a legal obligation on the state. The act empowers the poor, who can now demand work as a matter of right.

Poverty Policies in India

During the colonial era, the economic policies were based on the economic interest of the British rulers rather than on the people of the country. When India won its independence, the impact of colonized rule was already showing on all aspects of the Indian economy. India was left with high incidence of poverty and unemployment. The prevalence of unbridled poverty and unemployment required a welfare orientation in the public economic policy. In a nutshell, the social and economic challenges before the country were immense. Poverty reduction and providing basic needs to its people have been one the major aims of independent India. Decades after independence, India is still struggling to address the issue of poverty. This is evident from the fact that India is ranked 130 among 188 countries in the Human Development Index(HDI)[4]. Despite India's booming economy, which is now 10th largest in the world,302 million people (21.8percent of the total population) were living below the poverty line[5] in 2004-05(61st NSSO round)[6]. According to the Human development Report(HDR) 2003, of the United Nations Development Programme, India has the largest number of poor among the countries of the world and is the home to one-fourth of the world's poor[7].

Indian government has been taking up various measures to overcome the problem of poverty. Various poverty alleviation programmes comprising of wage employment programmes, rural housing schemes and a public distribution system were initiated from time to time. Some programmes were successful to some extent in addressing the issue of poverty whereas others suffered from major flaws in its implementation.

Till 1960s, there were no strong steps taken up to address the issue of rural poverty. The rural sector was neglected which resulted in agricultural stagnation by the harvest failure in 1966. The government of India gave a serious thought in the Fourth Five Year Plan with its focus to raise the standard of living of the people, especially of the less privileged sections of society. With its aim to remove inequality, the Government of India introduced, the Crash Scheme for Rural Employment (CSRE) in April, 1971. The scheme aimed to alleviate the prevailing conditions of unemployment and underemployment in rural areas, by generating additional employment through additional rural works. The other objective of CSRE was to generate assets of a durable nature in the areas of minor irrigation, land development, roads, afforestation, school buildings, etc. The evaluation study of CSRE, however, did not rate it as a successful programme. The reason for this, according to the study, was poor planning, organization and administration of the scheme. The use of labour contractors and unrealistic wages paid under the CSRE also created problems[8].

The experience of CSRE indicated the need for more concentrated efforts to tackle the problem of rural unemployment. The Bhagavati Committee[9] on "Rural Unemployment" drew attention to this aspect in its report, and recommended the initiation of the Pilot Intensive Rural Employment Project (PIREP) as an action-cum-research programme in rural areas. PIREP was introduced in 15 selected blocks in October, 1972 for a period of three years. Over and above employment generation, it also aimed at studying the nature and dimensions of the problem of unemployment among wage seeking rural workers. PIREP proved to be a slightly better programme in the sense that it threw light on certain characteristics of rural unemployment. However, it was not rated as successful by the review committee[10] on PIREP. The review committee pointed out that due to certain organizational problems, PIREP could not be of much use in evolving comprehensive programmes for the whole country.

In 1970-71, a Rural Works Programme was an attempt to mitigate the conditions of scarcity in drought prone areas. The programme was expected to provide work for an average of 100 days in a year for 2.5 million persons or more. The intention was to take up works taken up by state, local bodies and community level as projects under the programme. It also wanted to involve both unskilled and semi-skilled labour. Subsequently, it was realized that a mere rural works programme would not help in attaining these goals. The programme was sought to be reoriented on the basis of an area development approach and was re-designated as the Drought Prone Area Programme(DPAP) at the time of the mid-term appraisal of the Fourth Five Year Plan. The programme was confined to those areas which were originally taken up under the Rural Works Programme.

The Fifth Five Year Plan was drafted in late 1973 when the world economy was in a troublesome state. This had a negative impact on the Indian economy. Prices in the energy and food sector skyrocketed and as a consequence inflation became inevitable. The rising prices quickly forced a series of revisions. The plan was subsequently approved in late 1976 but was terminated at the end of five years (1977) because a new government wanted different priorities and programmes. Therefore, the five year plan was designed in a way to meet the needs of the time. The issues that were emphasized were to increase the level of employment, reduce poverty and to attain self sufficiency in agriculture.

In this backdrop, the Food for Work Programme(FFWP) was introduced in April,1977 as a non-plan scheme. As some surplus food stocks were available with government, it planned to use them in this employment programme. FFWP was implemented by the development administration directly, without any help from labour contractors. One special advantage of FFWP was its part wage payment in food grains at subsidized prices, which assured minimum food consumption and, therefore, minimum nutrition to the beneficiaries. FFWP was evaluated by the Programme Evaluation Organisation (PEO) of the Planning Commission[11]. It pointed out that the major problems of the programme pertained to its administration and implementation. FFWP continued till 1980.

The Small Farmer Development Agency (SFDA) and Marginal Farmers and Agricultural Labourer (MFAL) were started on a pilot basis with specific objectives of improving the economic conditions of small and marginal farmers and landless agricultural labourers to bring them into the main stream of economic development. The two schemes, SFDA and MFAL, were started with this objective of identifying the problems of small farmers for providing help to ensure availability of inputs, services and credit, preparation of appropriate programmes for making small and marginal farmers economically viable and for improving the lot of landless agricultural labourers by raising the output of small holdings and generating employment through subsidiary occupations.

Initially, 46 SFDA and 41 MFAL projects were started in the beginning of the Fourth plan and they were to continue for five years. The Fifth Five Year Plan after visualizing a lot of operational deficiencies in the working of SFDA and MFAL proposed to take a corrective measure for making requisite operational improvements and on the basis of recommendation of the National Commission of Agriculture, the two schemes were merged in the Fifth Five Year Plan and designated as SFDA.

Thus, the SFDA was the only organization at the district level charged solely with the responsibility of improving the economic conditions of the weaker sections of the society. However, in a study conducted by the Planning Commission, it was found that proper care was not exercised in the selection of some of the project areas and very little attention had been paid to the identification of agricultural labourers[12]. As a result of improper identification and verification of beneficiaries, the benefits of the schemes accrued to undeserving persons to the extent of about nine percent.

The National Rural Employment Programme (NREP) was formulated during the Sixth Five Year plan on the basis of the lessons learnt from previous public works programmes. It was an important part of the anti-poverty programme of the Sixth Plan. The basic objectives of the programme were generation of additional gainful employment for the unemployed and the underemployed men and women in the rural areas and creation of durable community assets to strengthen the rural infrastructure which would lead to a rapid growth of the rural economy, a steady rise in the income level of the rural poor and an improvement in their nutritional status and living standards. NREP was implemented as a centrally sponsored scheme, with the expenditure shared between the centre and the states on a 50:50 basis. The NREP, which had been launched with considerable enthusiasm, fell much behind its avowed goals. The Public Accounts Committee, commenting on its tragic plight, mentioned that the scheme had been launched in many areas without a proper survey undertaken of the scale and magnitude of rural employment, that the projects were not need-based and were stereotyped activities mainly relating to roads and other construction reminiscent of old famine relief works.

Despite the fact that NREP had been launched, it was felt that there was a need to tackle the problem of rural employment in a more direct and specific manner particularly during the lean agricultural periods when work was scare. Hence, the Rural Landless Employment Guarantee Programme (RLEGP) was launched in August, 1983. The basic objectives of the programme were:

- to improve and expand employment opportunities for the rural landless with a view to providing employment upto 100 days in a year for at least one member of every landless labour household;
- to create durable assets for strengthening the rural infrastructure.

The wages paid to the unskilled workers in this programme was notified by the state government under the Minimum Wages Act, 1948. Further, the wages paid were partly in cash and partly in kind (foodgrains).

The Integrated Rural Development Program (IRDP) was introduced in 1980.It is largely an asset endowment programme which provides a package of grant subsidy and credits to purchase a productive asset. It is based on the concept that the poor will be able to generate self-employment and thereby supplement their income through the assets distributed under the IRDP. The administrative unit of the IRDP is the block which typically consists of 10,000 villages and 60,000 to 100,000 persons. With a total investment of Rs.225 billion, the IRDP ranks as the largest rural development programme in India's history.

Though development of women as human resource was made a part of the IRDP, no significant results were achieved. Therefore, to provide specific alteration to the improvement of nutritional levels of women and children and also to improve their status, the scheme of Development of Women and Children in Rural Areas was implemented in 1982.The objective of the programme included assistance to individual women to enable her to make use of facilities provided under IRDP, provision of supportive services at the worksites and provision of childcare facilities.

The Training for Rural Youth for Self-Employment (TRYSEM) was initiated on 15 August, 1979 as a component of IRDP. Under this scheme, 40 rural youth between the ages of 18 and 35 in each block are given training in entrepreneurship and skills to assist them in self-employment vocations. Under TRYSEM, nearly 1 million youth were trained during the Sixth Plan period.

The Employment Guarantee Scheme (EGS) of Maharashtra operating since 1972 is a significant step in poverty alleviation programmes. The EGS of Maharashtra was different from other poverty alleviation programmes of the government. It guarantees work to all those who are willing to work at a fixed rate. It was intended to provide employment on productive works to the workers desirous of rendering unskilled manual work and thereby reduce the incidence of unemployment, under employment and poverty in rural areas. The State government gave statutory backing to the guarantee of employment through the Employment Guarantee Act, 1977. The guarantee of work is restricted to unskilled manual work. In 1983-84,164.5 million man-days of employment were reported to have been generated.

The United Nations development Programs (UNDP) Human Development Report (1993)[13] commends Maharashtra's EGS as one of the largest public programs in the developing world.EGS has been evaluated by a number of agencies. The reports show that in spite of various limitations, the programme has proved to be successful in terms of its impact on employment generation and the wage rate. It has been suggested, that the programme needs to be strengthened in the areas of planning and organization.

V.S. Page, founder of the EGS and president of the Maharashtra State Employment Guarantee opined that "A major problem of the EGS is the lack of discipline. Labourers need more discipline in applying for work, coming to work daily, and in showing up on time. The administration needs discipline to avoid corruption."[14]

The NREP and RLEGP were merged in April 1989(i.e. last year of the Seventh Plan) under the Jawahar Rozgar Yojana(JRY).The progamme was designed to generate meaningful employment opportunities for the unemployed and underemployed in rural areas through the creation of economic infrastructure and community and social assets. Initially, the JRY also included the Indira Awas Yojana(IAY) and the Million Wells Scheme(MWS) and later it was detached to make for separate schemes. Under JRY,73,764.83 lakh mandays of employment were generated till 1998-99 employment generation progressively declined over the years, partly due to lower central allocations in the Ninth Plan and partly due to increasing cost of creating employment.

A major proportion of JRY funds were spent on roads and buildings. Over 47percent of the employment generated benefited SC/STs. The village community found the assets created under the programme useful. However, against 40percent of the population in a village *panchayat* who sought work, only 15percent were actually employed.[15]

The Employment Assurance Scheme (EAS) was started in 2nd October, 1993 initially in 1,778 blocks of 261 districts. During 1994-95, the scheme was extended to 409 additional blocks which included the newly identified blocks under Drought Prone Areas Programme (DPAP), Desert Development Programme (DDP) and Modified Area Development Approach (MADA, having a larger concentration of tribal population).Subsequently, the scheme was extended to cover all the blocks by April 1997.The scheme aimed at providing assured employment of 100 days of unskilled manual works to the rural poor, who are in need of employment and seek it. The secondary objective is the creation of economic infrastructure and community assets for sustained production and employment generation. The assurance of 100 days of employment extends to men and women above 18 years and below 60 years of age, normally residing in the villages of the blocks covered by EAS.A maximum of two adults per family are to be provided assured employment of 100 days under the scheme, if and when they seek it during the lean season.

A comprehensive evaluation of the EAS by the Programme Evaluation Organisation[16] of the Planning Commission has revealed a number of flaws. The wage-material norm of 60:40 has not been observed. Genuine muster rolls have also not been maintained. Prescribed norms relating to the type of assets to be created (forty percent for watershed development and twenty percent each of minor irrigation link roads and buildings for schools and *anganwadis*) have not been followed.

The most important challenges in the Ninth Five Year Plan were to provide employment not only for the additions to the labour force during the plan period, but also to reduce the back-log of unemployment accumulated from the past. Keeping in view of the challenges, various programmes were launched.

Jawahar Gram Samridhi Yojana(JGSY) was launched in April,1999 by restructuring the Jawahar Rozgar Yojana and is implemented by Gram panchayats for creating productive community assets. The objective of JGSY was to create village infrastructure including durable assets to increase the opportunities for sustained employment for the rural jobless, preference being given to SC/ST families below the poverty line and physically challenged persons. In 1999-2000, JGSY provided 450.05(lakhs) man-days of employment[17]. In 1999-2000, the government decided to merge the various self-employment schemes in the rural sector (IRDP, DWCRA, TRYSEM, SITRA, MWS and GKY) into a single, all inclusive scheme called Swarna Jayanti Gram Swarozgar Yojana (SGSY).The objective of the SGSY is to establish a large number of micro-enterprises in the rural areas. Persons coming under the scheme will be known as *Swarozgaris*(self-employed) and not beneficiaries. Persons below the poverty line will be organized into Self Help Groups (SHGs) through the process of social mobilization, training and capacity building. They will be provided income-generating assets through a mix of bank credit and government subsidy. The scheme is being implemented on a cost-sharing ratio of 75:25 between the centre and the states. Since inception of the scheme upto December 31st, 2006, total funds of Rs.16, 433.66 crore were utilized to benefit 73.20 lakh *Swarozgaris*.

Pradhan Mantri Gramodaya Yojana(PMGY) was launched in 2000-01 in all States and the Union Territories in order to achieve the objective of sustainable human development at the village level. The PMGY envisages allocation of Additional Central Assistance to the States and Union Territories for selected basic minimum services in order to focus on certain priority areas of the government. PMGY initially had five components viz. primary health, primary education, primary shelter, rural drinking water and nutrition. Electrification has been added as an addition al component from 2001-02.

The Sampoorna Grameen Rozgar Yojana(SGRY) was launched in September,2001.The schemes of Jawahar Gram Samridhi Yojana(JGSY) and Employment Assurance Scheme(EAS) have been fully integrated with SGRY. The objective of the scheme is to provide additional wage employment along with food security, creation of durable community, social and economic assets and infrastructure development in the rural areas. The scheme envisages generation of 100 crore man-days of employment in a year. The cost of the programme is to be shared between the centre and the states on a cost sharing ratio of 75:25(including food grains component).In 2006-07, upto October 31st,2006,the number of person days of employment generated under SGRY was 18.41 crore.

Other than these, the National Food for Work Programme was launched on November 14, 2004 in 150 most backward districts of the country with the objective to intensify the generation of supplementary wage employment. The programme is open to all rural poor who are in need of wage employment and desire to do manual unskilled work. It is implemented as a 100percent centrally sponsored scheme and the food grains are provided to states free of cost. However, the transportation cost, handling charges and taxes on food grains are the responsibility of the states. The collector is the nodal officer at the district level and has the overall responsibility of planning, implementation, coordination, monitoring and supervision. In 2005-06, of the allocation of Rs.4, 500 crore and 15 lakh tones of foodgrains, Rs.2, 219 crore and 11.58 lakh tones of food grains had been released upto January 27th, 2006.

Based on the experiences of previous poverty alleviation and employment generation policies and a long drawn struggle by various sections of the people, MGNREGA was enacted in 2005 by the Government of India to fight poverty more effectively. During this period most of the developing countries were in distress from neo-liberal policies. As has been rightly put forward by Hirway et.al (2010) that the neoliberal policies have treated employment very indifferently, creating shortage of decent work opportunities in most developing countries. MGNREGA was enacted to reinforce the commitment towards livelihood security in rural areas[18].The significance of MGNREGA lies in the fact that it creates a right-based framework for wage employment programmes and makes the government legally accountable for providing employment to those who ask for it.

The Mahatma Gandhi National Rural Employment Guarantee Act, 2005

The pro-poor policy MGNREGA was not enacted in a wink. It was a long drawn struggle of many labour movements, social activists, researchers and academicians. It came to the mainstream policy debates in mid 2004. It started with the campaign for an Employment Guarantee in Rajasthan, as an extension of the employment- based drought relief programmes launched in 2001 and 2003.

It got impetus when the United Progressive Alliance led by Congress party took over the government in May, 2004. By that time, India was already committed to achievement of the Millennium Development Goals by signing the Millennium Declaration in September, 2000. The first goal was eradication of poverty and hunger. The enactment of the Act was in the agenda of the Congress Party during the elections. It was at the top of the list of National Common Minimum Programme (NCMP) of the UPA government. With support from the Left parties as alliance, the UPA moved forward with the enactment of the policy. The drafting of the MGNREGA was prepared by the National Advisory Council (NAC).After a long discussion, debates and revisions, the final draft was geared up as the National Rural Employment Guarantee Act, 2005 which was renamed as Mahatma Gandhi National Rural Employment Guarantee Act on the birth anniversary of Mahatma Gandhi in 2009. It is also known as the as the pet project of the Congress led United Progressive Alliance.

MGNREGA received the assent of the President of India on 5th September, 2005 and it was notified on 7th September, 2005. The Act says that " An Act to provide for the enhancement of livelihood security of the households in rural areas of the country by providing at least one hundred days of guaranteed wage employment in every financial year to every household whose adult members volunteer to do unskilled manual work and for matters connected therewith or incidental thereto".[19] It provides a statutory guarantee of wage employment and it is demand driven which ensures that employment is provided where and when it is most needed. The legal mandate of providing employment in a time bound manner is underpinned by the provision of Unemployment Allowance. The Act is designed to offer an incentive structure to the States for providing employment as ninety percent of the cost for employment provided is borne by the Centre. The right to work brings security in people's lives.

MGNREGA is a paradigm shift from wage employment programmes. Some of the significant aspects of this paradigm shift provided by the guidelines are given below:

I. MGNREGA provides a statutory guarantee of wage employment.

II. It provides a rights-based framework for wage employment. Employment is dependent upon the worker exercising the choice to apply for registration, obtain a Job Card, and seek employment for the time and duration that the worker wants.

III. There is a 15 day time limit for fulfilling the legal guarantee of providing employment.

IV. The legal mandate of providing employment in a time bound manner is underpinned by the provision of Unemployment Allowance.

V. The Act is designed to offer an incentive structure to the States for providing employment as ninety percent of the cost for employment provided is borne by the Centre. There is a concomitant disincentive for not providing employment as the States then bear the double indemnity of unemployment and the cost of unemployment allowance.

VI. Unlike the earlier wage employment programmes that were allocation based. MGNREGA is demand driven. Resource transfer under MGNREGA is based on the demand for employment and this provides another critical incentive to States to leverage the Act to meet the employment needs of the poor.

VII. The public delivery system has been made accountable, as it envisages an Annual Report on the outcomes of MGNREGA to be presented by the Central Government to the Parliament and to the Legislature by the State Government. Specifically personnel responsible for implementing the Act have been made legally responsible for delivering the guarantee under the Act.

Objectives of the Act

The Act aims to enhance the livelihood security of the people in rural areas. As per the operational guidelines on MGNREGA provided by the Ministry of Rural Development, the objectives of the Act are:

I. Strong social safety net for the vulnerable groups by providing a fall-back employment source, when other employment alternatives are scarce or inadequate.

II. Growth engine for sustainable development of an agricultural economy. Through the process of providing employment on works that address causes of chronic poverty such as drought, deforestation and soil erosion, the Act seeks to strengthen the natural resource base of rural livelihood and create durable assets in rural areas.

III. Empowerment of rural poor through the processes of a rights-based Law.

IV. New ways of doing business, as a model of governance reform anchored on the principles of transparency and grass root democracy.

Salient Features of the Act

The salient features of the Act are as follows:

I. Adult members of a rural household, willing to do unskilled manual works, may apply for registration in writing or orally to the local *gram panchayat*.

II. The *gram panchayat* after due verification will issue a Job Card. The Job Card will bear the photograph of all adult members of the household willing to work under MGNREGA and is free of cost.

III. The Job Card should be issued within 15 days of application.

IV. A Job Card holder may submit a written application for employment to the *gram panchayat*, stating the time and duration for which work is sought. The minimum days of employment have to be at least fourteen days.

V. The *gram panchayat* will issue a dated receipt of the written application for employment, against which the guarantee of providing employment within 15 days operates.

VI. Employment will be given within 15 days of application for work, if it is not then daily unemployment allowance as per the Act, has to be paid liability of payment of unemployment allowance is of the States.

VII. Work should ordinarily be provided within 5 km radius of the village. In case work is provided beyond 5 km., extra wages of 10 percent are payable to meet additional transportation and living expenses.

VIII. Wages are to be paid according to the Minimum Wages Act 1948 agricultural labourers in the State, unless the Centre notifies a wage rate which will not be less than Rs.60/day. Equal wages will be provided to both men and women.

IX. Wages are to be paid according to piece rate or daily rate. Disbursement of wages has to be done on weekly basis and not beyond a fortnight in any case.

X. At least one-third beneficiaries shall be women who have registered and requested work under the scheme.

XI. Worksite facilities such as crèche, drinking water, shade have to be provided.

XII. The shelf of projects for a village will be recommended by the *gram sabhas* and approved by the *zilla panchayat*.

XIII. At least 50 percent of works will be allotted to *gram panchayat* for execution.

XIV. Permissible works predominantly include water and soil conservation, afforestation and land development works.

XV. A 60:40 wage and material ratio has to be maintained. No contractors and machinery is allowed.

XVI. The central government bears the 100 percent wage cost of unskilled manual labour and 75 percent of the material cost including the wages of skilled and semi skilled workers.

XVII. Social audit has to be done by the *gram sabha.*

XVIII. Grievance redressal mechanisms have to be put in place for ensuring a responsive implementation process.

XIX. All accounts and records relating to the Scheme should be made available for public scrutiny.

Stakeholders

The roles and responsibilities of stakeholders in the implementation of the Act are discussed at different levels.

Village Level

Wage Seekers

The wage seekers are the primary stake holders of the Act. Their exercise of choice to demand employment is the trigger of key processes. The rights of the wage seekers includes application for registration, obtaining a Job Card, application for work, choice of time and duration of the work applied for. There is provision of work to be provided within 15 days of application and provide Unemployment Allowances in case employment is not provided within 15 days of submitting the application or from the date when work is sought. The wage seekers also have the right to check their Muster Rolls and to get information regarding their employment entered in their Job Cards.

Gram Sabha

The *gram sabha* will recommend works to be taken up under NREGS. It will conduct social audits on implementation of the Scheme. Further, the *gram sabha* is to be used extensively as a forum for sharing information about the Scheme.

Gram Panchayat

In the implementation of the Act, *gram panchayat* plays a pivotal role at the village level. The gram panchayat will be responsible for

- planning of works,
- receiving applications for registration,
- verifying registration applications,
- registering households,

- issuing Job Cards,
- receiving applications for employment,
- issuing dated receipts,
- allotting employment within 15 days of application,
- executing works,
- maintaining records,
- convening the *gram sabha* for social audit,
- monitoring the implementation at the village level.

Block Level

Intermediate Panchayat

The intermediate *panchayat* will be responsible for the consolidation of the *gram panchayat* plans at the block level and for monitoring and supervision.

Programme Officer

The programme officer essentially acts as a coordinator for NREGS at the block level. The chief responsibility of the programme officer is to ensure that anyone who applies for work gets employment within 15 days.

The other important functions of programme officers are as follows:

- Scrutinizing the annual development plan proposed by the *gram panchayats*.
- Including the proposals of the intermediate panchayat.
- Consolidating all proposals into the block plan and submitting it to the intermediate panchayat.
- Matching employment opportunities with the demand for work at the block level,
- Disposal of complaints
- Ensuring that social audits are conducted by the *gram sabhas* and following up on them.
- Payment of unemployment allowance in case employment is not provided on time.

District Level

District Panchayats

District *panchayats* will be responsible for finalizing the district plans and the labour budget and for monitoring and supervising the Employment Guarantee Scheme in the district.

District Programme Coordinator(DPC)

The State government will designate a district programme coordinator, who can be either the Chief Executive Officer of the district panchayat or the District Collector or any other district level officer of appropriate rank. The overall responsibility of the DPC is to ensure that the scheme is implemented according to the Act at the district level. In addition the DPC is responsible for information dissemination, training, consolidating block plans into a district plan, release and utilization of funds. The DPC has to ensure that administrative and technical approvals to the shelf of projects have been accorded on time. The monitoring of works, verification of muster rolls and submission of monthly progress report is also the responsibility of the DPC.

State Level

State Employment Guarantee Council (SEGC)

A State Employment Guarantee Council (State Council) has to be set up by every State Government under Section 12 of MGNREGA. The SEGC shall advise the State Government on the implementation of the scheme and evaluate and monitor it. It is the role of SEGC to decide on the 'preferred works' to be implemented under NREGS and recommend the proposals of works to be submitted to the Central Government under Schedule I Section 1(ix) of the Act. It will also prepare an annual report on the implementation of the NREGS in the State to be presented to the State Legislature.

The responsibilities of the State Government in the implementation of MGNREGA are as follows:

- Wide communication of the scheme
- Setting up the SEGC
- Establishing a State Employment Guarantee Fund
- Ensuring that full time dedicated personnel are in place for implementing MGNREGA, specially the gram panchayat assistant (*Gram Rozgar Sahayak)* and the Programme Officer, and the technical staff
- Ensuring that the State share of NREGS budget is released on time
- Delegation of financial and administrative powers to the District Programme Coordinator and Programe Officer,

as is deemed necessary for effective implementation of the scheme

- Training
- Establishing a network of professional agencies for technical support and for quality control measures
- Regular review, monitoring and evaluation of NREGS processes and outcomes.
- Ensuring accountability and transparency in the scheme at all levels.

Central Level

Central Employment Guarantee Council (CEGC)

A Central Employment Guarantee Council (Central Council) has been set up under the chairmanship of the Minister of Rural Development. The Central Council is responsible for advising the Central Government on MGNREGA related matters, and for monitoring and evaluating the implementation of the Act. It will prepare Annual Reports on the implementation of MGNREGA for submission to Parliament.

Ministry of Rural Development (MORD)

The Ministry of Rural Development is the nodal Ministry for the implementation of MGNREGA. It is responsible for ensuring timely and adequate resource support to the States and to the Central Council. It has to undertake regular review, monitoring and evaluation of processes and outcomes. It is responsible for maintaining and operating the Management Information System to capture and track data on critical aspects of implementation, and assess the utilization of resources through a set of performance indicators. It will support innovations that will help in improving processes towards the achievement of the objectives of the Act. It will support the use of Information Technology (IT) to increase the efficiency and transparency of the processes as well as improve interface with the public. It will also ensure that the implementation of MGNREGA at all levels is sought to be made transparent and accountable to the public.

Process of Employment

The Mahatma Gandhi National Rural Employment Guarantee Scheme (MGNREGS) is open to all rural households in the areas notified by the Central Government. The entitlement of 100 days of guaranteed employment in a financial year is in terms of a household. This entitlement of 100 days per year can be shared within the household; more than one person in a household can be employed (simultaneously or at different times).

All adult members of the household who register may apply for work. To register, they have to:

I. Be local residents: 'Local' implies residing within the Gram panchayat. This includes those that may have migrated some time ago but may return

II. Be willing to do unskilled manual work

III. 'Household' will mean a nuclear family comprising mother, father, and their children, and may include any person wholly or substantially dependent on the head of the family. Household will also mean a single-member family.

Application for Registration

The application for registration may be given on plain paper to the local *gram panchayat*. It should contain the names of those adult members of the household who are willing to do unskilled manual work, and particulars such as age, sex and SC/ST status. An individual may appear personally and make an oral request for registration. Verification of applications will be regarding local residence in the *gram panchayat* concerned, the household as an entity, and the fact that applicants are adult members of the household.

Notwithstanding the method of application, registration and verification suggested above, a *gram sabha* shall be convened when the Act commences in a district. The purpose of the *gram sabha* will be to explain the provisions of the Act mobilize applications for registration and conduct verifications. A door-to-door survey may also be undertaken to identify persons willing to register under the Act. The survey may be conducted by a team headed by the President of the *gram panchayat* and involving Ward members, SC/ST and women residents, a village-level government functionary and the *gram panchayat* Secretary. The team members may be given orientation at the Block/District level.

To allow maximum opportunities to families that may migrate, registration will be open throughout the year at the *gram panchayat* office during working hours. The process of verification shall be completed as early as possible, and in any case, not later than a fortnight after the receipt of the application in the *gram panchayat*. After verification, the *gram panchayat* will enter all particulars in the

Registrations Register in the *gram panchayat*.

Every registered household will be assigned a unique registration number. The registration number shall be assigned in accordance with a coding system similar to that prescribed by the Central and State Governments for the BPL Census 2002.Copies of the registration will be sent to the Programme Officer for the purpose of reporting to the Intermediate *panchayat* and District *panchayat* for further planning, tracking and recording. This must be done immediately, so that the Programme Officer has a consolidated record of likely demand to enable him/ her to organize resources accordingly. A *gram sabha* of registered workers must be held.

If a person who applies for registration turns out to have submitted incorrect information regarding his/her name, residence or adult status, he/she will become ineligible. In such cases, the *gram panchayat* will refer the matter to the Programme Officer. The Programme Officer, after independent verification of facts and giving the concerned person an opportunity to be heard, may direct the *gram panchayat* to cancel such registration and Job Card. Such cancellation lists will have to be made public and should be presented to the *gram sabha*.

Job Cards

The *gram panchayat* will issue Job Cards to every registered household. The timely issue of well-designed Job Cards is essential; this is a critical legal document, which also helps to ensure transparency and protect labourers against fraud. The job card should be issued immediately after verification, i.e. within a fortnight of the application for registration. Job cards should be issued in the presence of the local community. Photographs of adult members who are applicants have to be attached to the job cards. The cost of the job cards, including that of the photographs, will be borne as part of the programme cost. The State Government in a particular area may order the photograph to be affixed later (but not later than a month) if the immediate provision of a photograph is not possible. No photograph, name or details of any person other than that of the registered adult members of the household to whom that job card belongs shall be affixed or recorded in the job cards.

The Job Card will be in the custody of the household to whom it is issued and shall be valid for a period of five years and will have provision for the addition/deletion of members eligible to work. Deletions in any household on account of demise, or permanent change of residence of a member, are to be reported immediately by the household concerned. Additions desired may be applied for by the household. The *gram panchayat* will also undertake an annual updating exercise in the same manner as registration, the time for which should be fixed keeping in mind the work and migration season of the local workforce.

All additions and deletions made in the Registrations Register will be read out in the *gram sabha*.

The *gram panchayat* will send a list of additions/deletions to the Programme Officer. The Performa of the Job Card should be such that it contains permanent information regarding the household as well as the employment details for five years. Permanent information will include the household registration number and particulars (such as age and sex) of all adult members of the family who are willing to work. A cardholder may apply for a duplicate Job Card if the original card is lost or damaged. The application will be given to the *gram panchayat* and shall be processed in the manner of a new application, with the difference being that the particulars may also be verified using the duplicate copy of the Job Card maintained by the *panchayat*.

If a person has a grievance against the non-issuance of a Job Card, he/she may bring the matter to the notice of the Programme Officer. If the grievance is against the Programme Officer, he/she may bring it to the notice of the District Programme Coordinator or the designated grievance-redressal authority at the Block or District level. All such complaints shall be disposed off within 15 days.

Application for Work

Applications for work should generally be submitted to the *Gram panchayat*. In addition, as prescribed by the Act (Schedule II, Section 9), workers should have the option of submitting an application directly to the Programme Officer, but this should be treated as a 'fallback' option only.

Applications should be given in writing and should include:

- the registration number of the Job Card;
- the date from which employment is required; and
- the number of days of employment required.

The Application for employment may be on plain paper or it may be in a printed performa that will be made available free of cost at the *Gram panchayat*. A single application may be given for a number of days in different periods during the year for which employment is required. 'joint applications' may also be submitted by several applicants. The applicant may present himself in the *Gram panchayat* office to indicate willingness for work. This will be recorded by *Gram Rozgar Sahayak* in the prescribed application form and employment register. A worker having a job card may apply for work on work-site. His name may be entered in the Muster Roll by the Mate. *Gram Rozgar Sahayak* may make corresponding entries in the application form. This will encourage workers to get work without having to formally articulate their demand for work. The lack of formal application form should not be a ground for denying work. This is also the spirit of the law. A dated receipt for the application for work must be issued to the applicant. The application form for employment should have a counterfoil receipt on which the date can be entered and the dated receipt can then be issued immediately upon the submission of the application for employment. A format for application for employment with a dated receipt is at annexure 1A. All applications for employment must be entered in the Employment register as prescribed in these guidelines. Information on new applications for work shall be conveyed at least once a week by the *gram panchayat* to the Programme Officer.

Time Bound Employment

The *gram panchayat*/Programme Officer shall be responsible for providing wage employment to the applicant within 15 days of the date of receipt of the application in the case of advance applications, employment will be provided from the date that employment has been sought, or within 15 days of the date of application, whichever is later.

If a *Gram panchayat* is unable to provide employment within 15 days, it will be the responsibility of the Programme Officer to do so. The employment allotted by the Programme Officer will be intimated to the *gram panchayat* and vice versa. If upon receiving a request for work, an implementing agency directed by the Programme Officer does not start work on time, or does not employ the persons directed to it for work by the *gram panchayat*, the Programme Officer will make alternative arrangements to ensure employment for those applicants.

Choice of Works

The Schedule I, Para 1 lists of the Act list the permissible works in their order of priority as:

I. Water conservation and water harvesting;

II. Drought proofing (including afforestation and tree plantation);

III. Irrigation canal including micro and minor irrigation works;

IV. Provision of irrigation facility to land owned by households belonging to the Scheduled Castes and Scheduled Tribes or to land of beneficiaries of land reforms or that of the beneficiaries under the Indira Awas Yojana of the Government of India;

V. Renovation of traditional water bodies including desilting of tanks;

VI. Land development;

VII. Flood control and protection works including drainage in water logged areas;

VIII. Rural connectivity to provide all-weather access; and

IX. Any other work which may be notified by the Central Government in consultation with the State Government.

Para (iv) of Schedule I permits work on individual land "provision of irrigation facility to land owned by households belonging to the Scheduled Castes and Scheduled Tribes or to land of beneficiaries of land reforms or that of the beneficiaries under the Indira Awas Yojana of the Government of India".

This was amended to include horticulture plantation, land development and Below Poverty Line families vide Notification dated March 6, 2007 i.e. "provision of irrigation facility, horticulture plantation and land development facilities on land owned by households belonging to the Scheduled Castes and the Scheduled Tribes or to Below Poverty Line families or to beneficiaries of land reforms or to the beneficiaries under the Indira Awas Yojana of the Government of India".

This was further amended vide Notification dated July 24, 2009 to add small and marginal farmers i.e. "provision of irrigation facility, horticulture plantation and land development facilities to land owned by households belonging to the Scheduled Castes and the Scheduled Tribes or below poverty line families or to beneficiaries of land reforms or to the beneficiaries under the Indira Awas Yojana of the Government of India.

MGNREGA thus provides an opportunity for the households from SC/ST/ BPL families, beneficiaries of land reforms /IAY and of SF/ MF to take up land development, irrigation facility, and horticulture plantation on their land to mitigate drought, enhance agricultural productivity and generate steady income.

Planning and Execution of Works

Planning is critical to the successful implementation of the National Rural Employment Guarantee Scheme (NREGS). A key indicator of success is the timely generation of employment within 15 days while ensuring that the design and selection of works are such that good quality assets are developed. The need to act within a time limit necessitates advance planning. The basic aim of the planning process is to ensure that the District is prepared well in advance to offer productive employment on demand.

Development Plan

Section 16 (3) (4) of the Act states that every *gram panchayat* shall prepare a development plan and maintain a shelf of works and forward it to the Programme Officer for scrutiny and preliminary approval prior to the commencement of the year in which it is proposed.

The Development Plan is an Annual Work Plan that should comprise a shelf of projects for each village with administrative and technical approvals so that works can be started as soon as there is a demand for work. The Development Plan will be like a rolling plan, since the approved shelf of projects may carry over from one financial year to the next. The Development Plan will include the following components:

I. Assessment of labour demand

II. Identification of works to meet the estimated labour demand

III. Estimated Cost of works and wages

IV. Benefits expected in terms of employment generated and physical improvements (water conservation, land productivity)

Panchayat Raj Institutions Planning Process

Section 13 of MGNREGA makes the *Panchayats* at district, intermediate and village levels, the principal authorities for planning. The process of planning as laid down under the Act gives under

Section 16 of the Act, the power to make recommendations on the works to be taken up under MGNREGA to the *gram sabha* and the power to prepare a development plan comprising a shelf of projects on the basis of these recommendations of the *gram sabha* to the *gram panchayat*. The *gram panchayat* has to forward the development plan with its priorities to the Programme Officer for preliminary scrutiny and approval prior to the commencement of the year in which it is proposed to be executed. The Programme Officer has to consolidate the *gram panchayat* proposals and the proposals of the Intermediate *panchayat* into a block plan and after the approval of the Intermediate *panchayat*, forward it to the District Programme Coordinator. The District Programme Coordinator will consolidate the Block Plans and proposals from other implementing agencies and the District *Panchayat* will approve the block wise shelf of projects.

The sequence of approvals laid down under the Act necessitates time bound coordination between different levels so that the spirit and intent of the Act is maintained specially in terms of maintaining the works priorities. It is therefore legally imperative that there are no delays in the approval of the plan of works at any level and equally necessary to ensure that the priorities of the *gram sabha* are maintained. The absence of an approved shelf of projects affects the pace at which employment demand has to be met. Delay in finalising the plan of works will affect the finalization of the Labour Budgets by December, which in turn will affect fund release. It is necessary to ensure timely scrutiny and approval at each level, so that an adequate number of works with administrative and technical approvals are available to meet the demand for employment. It is also necessary to ensure that each level of approval maintains the order of priority between different works that is indicated in the development projects forwarded by the *gram panchayat* under Section 16(4).

The District Programme Coordinator will have overall responsibility for ensuring that the process of identification of works, their consolidation, and final approval of the shelf of projects is completed by December of the year preceding the financial year in which the shelf of works are to be executed. The works so finalised will be accorded technical and administrative approval and will constitute the shelf of projects for the next financial year.

At the block level, the Programme Officer (PO) will be responsible for ensuring that the *gram sabhas* are held on 2nd October of each year for identification and recommendations of works. The priority in which the works have to be taken up must also be mentioned in the resolution of the *gram sabha*. A copy of the resolution of the *gram sabha* recommending the works to be taken up in the following financial year and their priority will be sent to the Programme Officer. The Programme Officer will also be responsible for ensuring that the *gram panchayat* approves and consolidates all *gram sabha* recommendations into the village shelf of projects and submits it to the Intermediate *panchayat* within fifteen days of receiving all the *gram sabha* recommendations. All the *gram panchayat* development plans must reach the Programme Officer by October 15th.

Once all the *gram panchayat* Plans have been received, the Programme Officer will scrutinize the *gram panchayat*'s Development Plan for its technical feasibility. The Programme Officer will not reject a work proposed by the *gram panchayat*. If the proposal is not within the parameters of the Act, or appears technically unfeasible, the Programme Officer will return it to the *gram panchayat* for it to replace it with a valid proposal. The Programme Officer will consolidate all *gram panchayat* proposals into a Block plan and submit it to the Intermediate *Panchayat*. This entire process of scrutiny, re-reference to *gram panchayat*, if necessary, and consolidation and submission to the Intermediate *panchayat* will be completed by the Programme Officer by November 15th. The Intermediate *Panchayat* will maintain the priority among different works indicated by the *gram panchayats*. It is possible that there may be a need for works that involve more than one *gram panchayat*. Only such works will be included by the Intermediate *Panchayat*. The Intermediate *Panchayat* will not include works that are limited in their scope to an area within the jurisdiction of one *gram panchayat*. The Intermediate *panchayat* will approve the Block Plan within fifteen days of the submission by the Programme Officer and the Programme Officer will submit the Block Plan to the District Programme Coordinator by November 30th.

The District Programme Coordinator will scrutinize the Block plans, examining the appropriateness and adequacy of works in terms of likely demand as well as their technical and financial feasibility. He/she will also invite and examine work proposals from other implementing agencies, but in doing so, the priorities of the *gram panchayat* and the priorities of inter *gram panchayat* works as indicated in the Block Plan by the Intermediate *panchayats* will be maintained. The District Programme Coordinator will be responsible for consolidating the Block plans within a month of receiving all the Block Plans. The District Programme Coordinator will also formulate the labour budget on the basis of the district plan to indicate the amount of funds required to implement the scheme in the next financial year. The District Programme Coordinator will submit the Block wise shelf of projects and the labour budget based on it to the District *panchayat* by 15th December. The District *panchayat* will approve the Block wise shelf of projects and the labour budget by December 31st. The District Plan will comprise a Block-wise shelf of projects. The block wise shelf of projects will be arranged *gram panchayat* wise. The implementing agency for each work has to be identified keeping in view the mandatory minimum 50 per cent of the works to be executed by the *gram panchayat*. *Gram panchayat* may be given more than the minimum stipulated 50 percent.

The District Programme Coordinator will coordinate the preparation of detailed technical estimates and sanctions. The project report of each approved work shall contain all details as may be specified in the technical/works manual of the State Government. It will also clarify the expected outcomes such as person days of employment, specifications of the physical assets (e.g. length of road, size of a tank) and enduring outcomes (e.g. area irrigated, villages connected).The District Programme Coordinator will communicate the sanctioned Plan to the Programme Officer. The Programme Officer will forward a copy of the Block Plan with the shelf of projects to be executed in each *gram panchayat* as well as projects that may be inter *gram panchayat*. These will carry full project cost, time frame, person-days to be generated and the name of the implementing agency. Planning for projects must give priority to low-wage areas, where the demand for work at minimum wages is likely to be large. This process must be completed by December of the preceding year. The District Programme Coordinator will forward the Labour Budget to the State Government which will in turn, forward it with its recommendation to the Ministry of Rural Development by 31st January to enable it to release the Central share of funds for implementing the NREGS. This entire exercise has to be undertaken and completed by 31st December of the year proceeding the year for which the shelf of projects and the labour budget are being formulated. If a level fails to approve the plan proposal within the time limit indicated above, it will be deemed to be approved. In case the *gram panchayat* does not approve the *gram sabha* proposals within the time limit of October 15th, the Programme Officer will have the right to satisfy himself/herself on the basis of the copy sent to the Programme Officer office of the recommendations of the *gram sabha*, that the recommendations made are in accordance with the provisions of the Act and proceed to consolidate them into the Block Plan. If the Intermediate *panchayat* does not approve the Block Plan submitted by the Programme Officer by November 30th days it will be deemed to be approved and the Plan will be submitted by the Programme Officer to the District Programme Coordinator. If the District *panchayat* does not approve the Block wise shelf of Projects and the Labour Budget by 31st December, it will be deemed to have been approved. The District Programme Coordinator will have to proceed to communicate the approved shelf of projects to the Programme Officer and the *gram panchayats*. The District Programme Coordinator will also forward the Labour Budget to the State Government for further action. The Development Plan will provide the basis of the district's annual Labour Budget.

Financing Pattern

The financing pattern of NREGS has been distributed between the Central government and the State government. The Central Government will bear the following costs:

- The entire cost of wages for unskilled manual workers
- 75 percent of the cost of material and wages for skilled and semi-skilled workers.
- Administrative expenses as may be determined by the Central Government. These will include, inter alia, the salary and allowances of Programme Officers and their support staff and work site facilities
- Administrative expenses of the Central Employment Guarantee Council.
- The State Government will bear the following costs:
- 25 percent of the cost of material and wages for skilled and semi-skilled workers.
- Unemployment allowance payable in case the State Government cannot provide wage employment within 15 days of application.
- Administrative expenses of the State Employment Guarantee Council.

Employment Guarantee Funds

A National Employment Guarantee Fund has been set up by the Central Government to be managed according to the Rules made for this purpose. The grants to State Governments or Districts for implementation of MGNREGA shall be released from this Fund. The State Government may, by notification, establish a fund to be called the State Employment Guarantee Fund. This Fund is to be expended and administered as a Revolving Fund, with Rules that govern and ensure its utilization according to the purposes of the Act. Similar Revolving Funds should be set up under NREGS at the District, Block, and *gram panchayat* levels.

The State Government will design a complete Financial Management System for the transfer and use of funds. This must ensure transparency, efficiency and accountability, and track the use of funds towards the final outcomes. Separate bank accounts shall be opened for funds under the Scheme at the State, District and Block levels. The accounts shall be opened in public sector banks. Funds allocated to NREGS should not be used for other purposes under any circumstances.

Labour Budget

Chapter IV, Para 14, sub section (6) of the NREG Act says that the District Programme Coordinator shall prepare in the month of December every year a labour budget for the next financial year containing the details of anticipated demand for unskilled manual work in the district and the plan for engagement of labourers in the works covered under the Scheme. The Ministry of Rural Development will estimate the requirement of funds on the basis of projections made in the Labour Budget. Central funds will be sanctioned after examining these Labour Budgets and taking into account utilization of funds previously released.

Based on the assessment of labour demand, identification of works to meet this demand and estimated cost of works and wages, in the *gram panchayat* Development Plans, the district should formulate and approve the Labour Budget. The Labour Budget will be based on a realistic estimate for the number and kind of works to be taken up, as derived from the annual shelf of projects in the Development Plan. Labour Budgets should be submitted to the Government of India latest by January 31 each year for the next financial year. State Secretaries should ensure timely submission of Labour Budgets for all MGNREGA districts in their States to avoid delay in fund release. For this, it is important that the district follow time bound coordination at each level in the planning process from *gram panchayat* to District *panchayat*.

Estimate of labour should be realistic and close to actual achievement trends of the previous year in terms of households demand, days of employment demanded and expenditure. If a sharp rise in the employment demand is estimated, a proper justification for this should be clearly presented by the district in a narrative form along with the Labour Budget. The projected demand should be subsequently validated by actual trends in the months for which estimated have been made. If the actual monthly achievements do not corroborate (they may be less or higher than the estimates) this difference must be reviewed and analyzed at the district level.

An Empowered Committee, under the Secretary Rural Development, will appraise and approve the district Labour Budgets in consultation with the State Secretaries. State Labour Budgets received in the Ministry will be examined and issues, if any, will be communicated to the State for clarification/review. The States would be expected to respond to the issues raised so that the Labour Budget may be processed. The Empowered Committee will take a decision on the amount to be sanctioned.

Maintenance of Funds by the Gram Panchayat

Each *gram panchayat* will have a single bank account for the purpose of implementing NREGS works. This NREGS account will be operated jointly by the President and the Secretary of the *gram panchayat*. All payments made from the NREGS account will be reported to the *gram panchayat* at its next meeting and approval will be obtained. Any objection will be recorded and a copy of the minutes will be sent immediately to the Programme Officer for necessary action. Funds from the NREGS account may be spent on NREGS works after only these works have received the required Administrative and Technical Sanction from the competent authorities. The President of the *gram panchayat* will be personally liable for any expenditure made without such sanctions.

The NREGS-related accounts of the *gram panchayat* shall be presented for scrutiny at the biannual social audits of the *gram sabha*, in pre-specified formats. NREGS funds at the *gram panchayat* level cannot be used for other purposes under any circumstances. The *gram panchayat* President and Secretary shall be responsible for ensuring that disbursements from the NREGS account are made for legitimate purposes. Any diversion of NREGS funds will be treated as a defalcation and recovery proceedings will be immediately initiated. The *gram panchayats* will be authorized to spend the money released to them on the works that have been sanctioned for them to execute. After 60 percent of the allocation given to any *gram panchayat* has been spent, the *gram panchayat* may apply to the Programme Officer/DPC for release of additional funds. The proposal of the *gram panchayat* shall be accompanied by a statement of work-wise expenditure together with the report of the Vigilance and Monitoring Committee duly approved by the *gram sabha*.

Monitoring and Evaluation

The *gram sabha* will monitor all the works at the village level as well as the employment provided to each person who has applied for work. It will also monitor the registration and issue of job cards and the timely payment of wages.

Vigilance and Monitoring Committees

For every work sanctioned under the Scheme, there should be a local Vigilance and Monitoring Committee (VMC) composed of members of the locality or village where the work is undertaken, to monitor the progress and quality of work while it is in progress. The VMC will comprise nine members. The *gram sabha* will elect the members of this Committee and ensure that SC/STs and women are represented on it. It should have at least 50 percent of members from among MGNREGA workers. The VMC should be elected for the period of one year by the *gram sabha*. The GP/Implementing Agency should apprise this Committee of estimates regarding the work, time frame and quality parameters. The Final Report of the Committee should be attached along with the Completion Certificate of the work, and should also be placed at the next meeting of the *gram sabha* in the Panchayat where work has been executed. A copy of the Report will also be sent to the Programme Officer and the District Programme Coordinator. The Programme Officer will be responsible for ensuring that local Vigilance and Monitoring Committees are constituted. VMC should be village specific and not work specific. It should facilitate the social audit by the *gram sabha*.

Local Beneficiary Committees may also be constituted for effective articulation of their entitlements and their access to information.

The *gram panchayat* will monitor works executed by other Implementing Agencies, muster rolls maintained by them at worksites, and the payments made.

The Intermediate *Panchayat* and the Programme Officer will monitor the registration of households, issue of Job Cards, employment demanded and provided, maintenance of muster rolls, unemployment allowances paid, social audits, flow of funds, timely and correct payment of wages, and progress and quality of works. The Programme Officer shall be responsible for sending all reports and returns to the District Programme Coordinator, who in turn shall send reports to the State and Central Governments.

The District *Panchayat* and the District Programme Coordinator will monitor all aspects of implementation, especially timely issue of Job Cards, provision of employment, social audits, and flow of funds, progress and quality of works.

The State Government will monitor the Scheme in all its aspects of implementation, specially, timely and correct payment of wages, timely payment of unemployment allowances and grievance redressal. The State Government will send consolidated reports and returns to the Central Government.

Central Government will establish a monitoring system through internal and external monitoring agencies. A central monitoring and evaluation system will be evolved by the Central Employment Guarantee Council.

At all the levels, the following aspects of NREGS will be monitored:

I. Effectiveness and outreach of IEC activities specially among the Job Card holders
II. Application for Registration and verification process for registration
III. Time taken to issue Job Cards
IV. Application for Demand
V. Issue of dated receipts
VI. Allocation of employment within fifteen days
VII. Maintenance of authentic updated Muster Rolls on work sites
VIII. Quality of work executed
IX. Measurement of work done and maintenance of measurement books
X. Timely and correct payment
XI. Entries in the Job Cards
XII. Maintenance of records prescribed under the Guidelines
XIII. Grievance redressal
XIV. Fund utilization
XV. Organisation of social audits

Monitoring Methods

The following targets are fixed for internal verification of works at the field level by the official functionaries to be achieved within a quarter. Hundred percent of works at the Block level;Ten percent of works at the District level and two percent at the State level. Verification and quality audit by external monitors must be taken up at the Central, State and District levels. For this purpose, National Quality Monitors (NQM) at the national level may be designated by the Ministry of Rural Development with the approval of the Central Council. Similarly, State Quality Monitors (SQM) at the State level may be designated by the State Government with the approval of the State Council. The District will also identify District Quality Monitors (DQM) with the approval of the State Government. The Central Government may draw up broad indicative terms of reference for use by States for the quality monitors. All programme implementation authorities—from the Programme Officer to the District and State levels—shall report regularly on the online MIS developed by the Central Ministry. Field visits, inspections and sample checks (internally and externally) must be undertaken on a regular basis to ensure comprehensive and continuous assessment of the Scheme.

Evaluation

The objective of MGNREGA is the 'creation of durable assets and strengthening the livelihood resource base of the rural poor' (Schedule I, Section 2). Investments made under MGNREGA are expected to generate employment and purchasing power, raise economic productivity, promote women's participation in the workforce, strengthen the rural infrastructure through the creation of durable assets, reduce distress migration, and contribute to the regeneration of natural resources. Thus, outlays for NREGS have to be transformed into outcomes. Regular evaluations and sample surveys of specific NREGS works should be conducted to assess outcomes.

District-wise studies should be conducted or commissioned by the State Employment Guarantee Council. Block-wise evaluation studies should be conducted or commissioned by the District Programme Coordinator. SEGC should seek the association of research institutions of repute with this process. All evaluation agencies should be approved by SEGC. Broad guidelines for evaluation studies, including NREGS assessment criteria, should be framed by SEGC. SEGC should develop its own evaluation system in collaboration with research institutions of repute and review evaluations conducted by other agencies. The evaluation studies should also throw light on particular innovations in planning, monitoring or implementation. These should be sent to the State and Central Governments for examination and dissemination to other parts of the State and country.

The findings of the evaluation studies should be used by SEGC, the district *panchayats* and other institutions for initiating corrective action. The entitlements under the Act are legally justifiable. For this reason, among others, it is important to maintain accurate records of all aspects of implementation.

Transparency and Accountability

Transparency and accountability has been given utmost importance in the enactment of MGNREGA. For an effective implementation of the Act, the policy planners devised strategies to bring transparency and accountability in the policy.

Right to Information

The Right to Information Act should be followed both in letter and in spirit in all matters relating to MGNREGA. Section 4 of the Act, which concerns proactive disclosure of information, should be strictly complied with at all levels. Requests for copies of NREGS-related documents submitted under MGNREGA should be complied with within seven days. No request should be refused under any circumstances. In particular, no information should be withheld by invoking Clause 8 of the Right to Information Act. All MGNREGA-related information is in the public domain. Key documents related to MGNREGA should be proactively disclosed to the public, without waiting for anyone to 'apply' for them. A list of such key documents should be prepared by the State Employment Guarantee Council, and updated from time to time.

Public access to key records and key information should be ensured at all levels.

Updated data on demand received, registration, number of job cards issued, list of people who have demanded and been given/ not given employment, funds received and spent, payments made, works sanctioned and works started, cost of works and details of expenditure on it, duration of work, person-days generated, reports of local committees, and copies of muster rolls should be made public in a pre-designated format outside all offices of all agencies involved in implementing MGNREGA, and should also be placed by the *Gram panchayat* before the *gram sabha* once in every quarter. People should know who to apply to for information and for gaining access to records. There should be broad time limits for giving such information. The names and contact addresses of such key persons should be made known to the public. Fees charged for copies of MGNREGA-related documents should not exceed photocopying costs.

MGNREGA-related accounts of each *gram panchayat* should be proactively displayed and updated twice a year. Summary accounts should be displayed through various means, including painting on walls at the *Panchayat* Bhawan, postings on notice boards and publication in Annual Reports available at cost price.

Report Cards on local works, employment and funds should be posted by the *gram panchayat* on its premises and by the Programme Officer at the Intermediate *panchayat*/Programme Officer's office, and for the whole District by the District Programme Coordinator at the District Programme Coordinator/District *panchayat* office.

Financial Audit

Financial Audit is mandatory. This must be carried out at the end of the financial year by each District. The audit will be done either by Local Fund Auditors or by the Chartered Accountants appointed by the State Government. A copy of the Audit Note will be sent to the State Government. A concurrent audit will be undertaken in addition to this.

The Accountant General will also conduct the Audit of Accounts of MGNREGA in addition to the audit conducted by the Chartered Accountants. The audit team of the Accountant General shall be supplied with a copy of the audit conducted by the Chartered Accountants. The Audit Report of the Chartered Accountant and the Utilization Certificate for the previous year must be submitted latest by September next year by the District Programme Coordinator. If the Audit Report is not received, or if the observations of the Auditor and of the Ministry on the Audit Report are not properly attended to or complied with, to the satisfaction of the Ministry within the financial year, the Ministry will be within its right to stop the funds for the next financial year. The responsibility for payment of unemployment allowance arising out of the non-availability of funds for this reason shall be on the State Government.

Citizens' Charter

A model 'Citizens' Charter' should be developed covering all aspects of the duties of *panchayat* and officials under the Act. The Citizens' Charter should describe the specific steps involved in implementing the provisions of the Act, and lay down the minimum service levels mandated by these provisions on the *panchayats* and the officers concerned.

Grievance Redressal

I. The Programme Officer will be the Grievance Redressal Officer at the Block level, and the District Programme Coordinator at the District level.

II. A system of appeal will be designed to deal with grievances at each level. Appeal against the *gram panchayat* will be to the Programme Officer. Appeal against the Programme Officer will be to the District Programme Coordinator. Appeal against the District Programme Coordinator may be with an appropriate authority designated by the State Government.

III. Name and address of the petitioner, and nature and date of the petition, are to be entered in a register, which will be uploaded on to the Internet on a weekly basis.

IV. The person registering the grievance is to be given a receipt with number and date so that he/she can follow up the status of disposal of his/her grievance from a counter in the office of the Programme Officer and over the Internet using the receipt number.

V. Once a grievance has been disposed of, the date and nature of disposal should be communicated to the petitioner. These details are to be made available over the Internet.

VI. Data generated by classifying petitions are to be analysed each month for region and type so that it becomes a tool for identifying areas that require senior management attention and redesigning of systems.

VII. All grievances will be disposed of within the time limit prescribed in the Act.

VIII. Attention is drawn to grievances relating to items listed as 'Mandatory Agenda' for the Social Audit Forum in Chapter 11 Section 6 of these Guidelines.

IX. Grievance redressal performance of all authorities under the Act and these Guidelines are to be posted on the Internet on a weekly basis.

X. The *gram sabha* and the Social Audit Forum shall provide a forum for public hearings so that grievances may be quickly redressed.

XI. The State Government may designate an alternative Grievance Redressal Authority at the Block, District and State levels.

XII. The State Government may consider setting up a system of Ombudsman at the State and District levels, using people of proven integrity.

XIII. A Help Line may be set up for grievance redressal.

XIV. Action taken on the complaints received by the Programme Officer and the District Programme Coordinator shall be placed before the meetings of the Intermediate *panchayats* and the district *panchayats* respectively.

- State Governments will formulate rules for grievance redressal. In formulating Rules, the following measures must be incorporated Complaints may be submitted in writing or orally.
- Complaint boxes at conspicuous places in the offices of the Programme Officer and District Programme Coordinators must be installed to facilitate submission of complaints.
- Complaints shall be entered in the complaint register and disposed within the statutory time limit.
- The complainants must also be informed of the action taken in writing.
- Monitoring of disposal of the complaint must be done at the next higher level every month.
- There must be monthly disclosure of complaints in local newspapers.
- Setting up a toll free help line must be considered.
- A system of appeal must be considered.
- A State level Officer must be designated to monitor the disposal of complaints in the State.
- Wide publicity must be made for grievance redressal at all levels.
- Monthly Reports on complaints received and disposed must be sent from GP to PO to DPC to State to Government of India and will also be entered on line in predesigned formats to the Ministry.

XV. and in case Rules have been formulated, these measures may be included, if not done already.

Social Audit

An innovative feature of the Mahatma Gandhi National Rural Employment Guarantee Act is that it gives a central role to 'social audits' as a means of continuous public vigilance (MGNREGA, Section 17). The basic objective of a social audit is to ensure public accountability in the implementation of projects, laws and policies. One simple form of social audit is a public assembly where all the details of a project are scrutinized. However, 'social audit' can also be understood in a broader sense, as a continuous process of public vigilance. That is the sense in which the term is used in this chapter. To avoid confusion, the term 'Social Audit Forum' will be used here to refer to the periodic assemblies convened by the *gram sabha* as part of the process of social audit.

In this perspective, a social audit is an ongoing process through which the potential beneficiaries and other stakeholders of an activity or project are involved at every stage: from the planning to the implementation, monitoring and evaluation. This process helps in ensuring that the activity or project is designed and implemented in a manner that is most suited to the prevailing (local) conditions, appropriately reflects the priorities and preferences of those affected by it, and most effectively serves public interest.

In the context of MGNREGA, the process of social audit should include public vigilance and verification of the following 11 stages of implementation:

- Registration of families
- Distribution of job cards
- Receipt of work applications and issue of dated receipts
- Preparation of shelf of projects and selection of sites
- Development and approval of technical estimates and issuance of work order
- Allotment of work to applicants
- Execution of works and maintenance of muster rolls
- Payment of wages
- Evaluation of work
- Payment of unemployment allowance
- Mandatory social audit in the *gram sabha* (Social Audit Forum)

Apart from the ongoing process of social audit, there will be a mandatory review of all aspects of the social audit at the *gram sabha* meetings to be held at least once every six months for this purpose. At these 'Social Audit Forums' information will be read out publicly, and people will be given an opportunity to question officials, seek and obtain information, verify financial expenditure, examine the provision of entitlements, discuss the priorities reflected in choices made, and critically evaluate the quality of work as well as the services of the programme staff.

Thus, the Social Audit Forum will not only give people an opportunity to review compliance with the ongoing requirements of transparency and accountability, but will also serve as an institutional forum where people can conduct a detailed public audit of all MGNREGA works that have been carried out in their area in the preceding six months.

Studies on Evaluation of MGNREGA

In the initial phase of the implementation of the Act, the evaluation of the policy was based the official data of the Ministry of Rural Development. Drèze and Oldiges[20] present the outcomes of the Act in the initial two years (2006-08) of the Act. MGNREGA generated 90 crores (nearly one billion) person-days of employment in 2006-7, at a cost of about Rs. 9,000 crores. There are startling differences in the levels of MGNREGA employment between different states. Some state governments have clearly decided to "own" MGNREGA, and seized this opportunity to provide large-scale employment to the rural poor at the cost of the Central Government (which foots about 90 per cent of the bill). In other states, the whole programme is yet to take off. Rajasthan was the best performer among all major states in 2006-7 (in terms of employment generation per rural). Indeed, employment guarantee has been a lively political issue in Rajasthan for quite a few years, and the state also had a high level of preparedness for the Act, having organized massive public works programmes almost every year in living memory. Note, however, that the small state of Tripura in the North-East (not shown in the table) is doing even better than Rajasthan, with 87 days of MGNREGA employment per rural household in 2006-7. In both states, employment generation under MGNREGA is already quite close to the upper limit of "100 days per rural household". This is an unprecedented achievement in the history of social security in India. MGNREGA is also an important tool for social change particularly for women. It was found that the mandatory provision of crèche facilities at MGNREGA worksites has been brazenly ignored. It is alarming to find that some states are evidently paying less than the statutory minimum wage, in flagrant violation of the Act. The most glaring offender in this respect is none other than Rajasthan, where MGNREGA workers earned a meagre Rs. 51 per day on average in 2006-7, even though the statutory minimum wage was Rs. 73 per day.

As per the official data for the financial year 2011-12 provided by the website of the Ministry of Rural Development, the data indicates that till date (accessed on 23-5-12), 4.99 crore households have been provided employment[21]. It is also interesting to note that women's participation rate is quite high with 48.18 percent. In particular, it holds the powerful prospect of bringing major changes in the lives of women. Women's work participation rate has increased over the years. The wider acceptability of MGNREGA work derives from several factors: it is locally available, being government work there is regularity and predictability of working hours, less chance of work conditions being exploitative and work is considered socially acceptable and "dignified[22] It can revolutionize the rural livelihoods in India. It has been rightly put by Dutt et.al. that "a scheme such as this can also provide valuable insurance against the many risks faced by India's rural poor in their daily lives"[23]. On the similar line Ghosh said that "employment generation schemes, if imaginatively conceived and properly implemented, can have very substantial effects in terms of creating conditions for much higher levels of economic activity and therefore growth, especially in the rural areas"[24].

Chakraborty[25]'s analysis of the data provided by the Ministry of Rural Development reveals that the fund utilisation ratio remains as low as 51percent even after completion of one full year of operation of MGNREGA. It also indicates that the existing institutional arrangement in poorer states is not good enough to implement the MGNREGA in an effective manner. There is an urgent need for both vertical and horizontal coordination across levels of governments within the states. The *gram sabha* can play an active role in the planning, monitoring and supervision of projects. In many places, *panchayats* do not have the necessary capacity to manage the schemes and capacity building ought to take place at the *panchayat* level. He suggested that in assessing the demand for labour, *panchayat* level preparation of labour budgets would go a long way for effective implementation.

Shah[26] says that MGNREGA has the potential to provide a "big push" in India's region of distress. For MGNREGA to be able to realise its potential, the role of the civil society organization is critical. But this calls for a new self-aware, self-critical politics of fortitutde, balance and restraint.

Similarly Mehrotra[27] examines the performance of MGNREGA. The state-wise figures for person-days of employment generated per household as per the report of Ministry of Rural Development (2006-07 and 2007-08) show considerable variation across states. The highest number of person-days is for Rajasthan- 85 per household whereas in Uttar Pradesh (U.P.) it is only 32 days and in Bihar, 35 (2006-07). Since the incidence of poverty in U.P. and Bihar is high and this should have led to a demand for jobs, the poor performance of these states almost certainly reflects inadequate effectiveness in the field.

The first Monitoring report prepared by Samarthan[28] – Centre for Development Support in collaboration with Poorest Area Civil Society Programme was carried out study in six states of India i.e. Bihar, Chattisgarh, Jharkhand, Madhya Pradesh, Maharastra and Uttar Pradesh. Some of the major findings on the implementation of the Act are:

- There was low awareness among citizens, elected representatives and government officials (at levels below block) and this has been a major reason for the flaws in the implementation of the scheme.
- In most of the states Job Cards had not been distributed properly
- In places where the Job Cards had been provided, it was observed that there were a lot of anomalies. In most of the states it was observed that the Job cards were not being used.
- It was also observed that people were not applying for jobs.
- In some states where people did apply for jobs they were not receiving proper receipts.

According to the Act, 50 percent of the implementation work will be carried out by the PRIs. The Ministry of Rural Development claims that the village *panchayat*s are implementing close to 83 percent of total MGNREGA works while others including independent implementing agencies and block *panchayat*s are implementing around seventeen percent of works. A study conducted on 200 backward districts of MGNREGA by Planning Commission has revealed that in some of the 200 districts, *panchayat*s do not exist, or are non-functional and the *gram sabhas* which are required to choose the shelf of projects are dormant in some of the cases.

However, the CAG report revealed lapses in the implementation of the Act[29]. The key findings of the report are that the delivery of the MGNREGA has deteriorated significantly. There are two aspects to this. First, very small portions of the poor people who have sought jobs under the MGNREGA have actually received employment. In the period April 2006 to March 2007, 10 percent of all such applications received minimum wage job. Between April and December 2007, the number of actual beneficiaries has dropped to just 3.3percent of total job seekers registered under the scheme. Second, even within the beneficiaries, only a small minority received the full promised deal. Thus, the CAG's sample reported that the average employment per person under the scheme was 45 days in April 2006-March 2007, whereas this has dropped to just 38 days during April-December 2007.In addition, the CAG has reported that the MGNREGA is afflicted with corruption and mis-utilization of funds, as well as inefficiency and unreliable documentation in most of the districts covered by the study. The worst performance in this regard has come from the poorest States of Bihar, Orissa, Jharkhand and Uttar Pradesh. These are the very states that have the greatest need for a comprehensive rural employment scheme [30].

The much publicised CAG report has also found many flaws in the implementation of the Act. Some of the findings of CAG are given below[31]:

- The introductory *gram sabha* meeting at the time of commencement of the Act was not convened in 119 GPs in Andhra Pradesh, Assam, Chhattisgarh, Haryana, Himachal Pradesh, Jharkhand, Karnataka, Kerala, Manipur, Orissa, Uttar Pradesh and West Bengal.
- Door to door survey to identify persons willing to register was not conducted in 290 *gram panchayats*(GPs) in 19 states issued to all registered households in 74 GPs in 11 states
- Job cards were not issued to all registered households in 74 GPs in 11 states.
- In Orissa, in 1 GP, 13 job cards were found by DRDA officials to be lying with GP officials. In another GP, 21 cards were lying with the GP authorities and were issued at the instance of audit.
- In Haryana, in 5 test checked GPs, against 637 registered households, 968 households were reported to have been issued job cards; in addition, 72 minors had also been registered for doing manual work. Also, in 16 test-checked

GPs, photographs were not attached in 2,238 cases of job cards.

- In Manipur, job cards were issued without identification.
- In Tamil Nadu, in Cuddalore District, out of 1, 19,813 households, 1093 households had not been issued job cards as of March 2007.
- In Karnataka, in the two district of Davanagere and Gulbarga, out of the total registered households of 2.33 lakhs and 3.89 lakhs, only 1.55 lakhs and 2.01 lakhs households were issued job cards.

The CAG report summarizes "significant deficiencies" and their impact on MGNREGA implementation: "The main deficiency was the lack of adequate administrative and technical manpower at the block and GP levels. The lack of manpower adversely affected the preparation of plans, scrutiny, approval, monitoring and measurement of works, and maintenance of the stipulated records at the block and GP level. Besides affecting the implementation of the scheme and the provision of employment, this also impacted adversely on transparency, and made it difficult to verify the provision of the legal guarantee of 100 days of employment on demand. Planning was inadequate and delayed, which resulted in poor progress of works. Systems for financial management and tracking were deficient, with numerous instances of diversion/ misutilisation, and delay in transfer of State Share. Monthly squaring of accounts at different levels to maintain financial accountability and transparency was also not being done. Maintenance of records at the block and GP levels was extremely poor, and the status of monitoring, evaluation and social audit was also not up to the mark".

A study of four states (Gujarat, Madhya Pradesh, Maharashtra and Rajasthan) conducted by Disha[32] reveal that most of the respondents had low level of education which was an impediment in their awareness regarding the provisions of the Act. It was also found that there were common problems like lack of proper information, no Job Card made or only temporary Job Cards were made, photographs were taken for Job Cards and delayed application process for work. The average period of employment is around 39 days. However, the two districts of Rajasthan with 63 days in Dungarpur and 67 days in Udaipur are considered to be in a better position as compared to other states. Delay in payment of wages was a common phenomenon in all the districts. An analysis of the averages wages paid in the different types of work across districts shows that in many instances, the wages paid are even below the minimum agriculture wage level decided by the government (Rs. 50 per day for Gujarat, Rs. 73 for Rajasthan and Rs. 63 for Madhya Pradesh).

The All-India Report on evaluation of MGNREGA: A Survey of Twenty Districts carried out by Institute of Applied Manpower Research for the Planning Commission assessed the effectiveness of the Act[33]. The study revealed, 80percent of the households did not get the work within the stipulated 15 days time of demand for work in writing, neither were they paid unemployment allowance. An enquiry was also made to assess the impact of the scheme on the overall quality of life of the beneficiaries. Due to the income generation through this scheme, the numbers of beneficiaries at the low earning level are reduced to nearly half in size resulting this on the rise of households with marginally higher income.

The Second Administrative Reform Commission[34] has found that functioning of PRI was limited and very few selected *panchayat* chiefs and other functionaries were given training. This underscores the importance of building capability in the *panchayats* through appropriate training and orientation programmes. It has also found that in some states even though these institutions exist they have not been sufficiently empowered to implement such large schemes and it is the Collector who supervises the implementation of the Act. However the Ministry of Rural Development in its Report to the People has indicated that functionaries are trained at different levels[35]. Following are the details of the training provided:

- PRI Functionaries – 7.45 lakhs
- VMC members – 7.71 lakhs
- Technical Staffs – 21437(in nos.)

The Ministry of Rural development (MoRD) has developed a Professional Institutional Network (PIN) for steady, sustainable interventions that enhance the quality of the MGNREGA to undertake concurrent monitoring and appraisal, evaluation and impact assessment and research[36]. The Ministry entrusted Rural Technology and Business Incubator (RTBI) of IIT Madras to conduct the impact assessment study in the state of Tamil Nadu. Eight districts were selected on the basis of performance, size of the districts and implementation phases as per the guidelines given by the Ministry to PIN.

The study identified positive and negative aspects of the Scheme in the study area. The positive aspects are:

- The job within the village is rewarding.
- Ensures safety for rural women thereby making them employable-additional wealth to rural household
- Ensures gender equality in rural Tamil Nadu
- Involvement of Self Help Groups improves NREGS activities
- The negatives aspects have been identified as follows:
- Improper wor estimation with out considering soil texture,climate conditions,etc.
- Limitations of 100 days of employment to household.
- Poor infrastructure provisions like crèche, first aid,etc.
- *Panchayats* that witness heavy enrolments suggest the beneficiaries to work on alternate days.

A study with special focus on women was conducted by National Federation of Indian Women (NIFW) for Ministry of Rural Development[37]. The study was conducted in selected four districts which were Rajnandgaon(Chhattisgarh), Jhabua (Madhya Pradesh), Mayurbhanj(Orissa) and Cuddalore(Tamil Nadu). In all the districts it has been found that respondents were very optimistic about the importance of MGNREGA in their lives. It has also been found that women workers in all the districts were taking their wages directly. The major concern was the awareness level of the respondents who are illiterate and belong to economically poor class. They were unaware about the provisions of the Act. There were lack of worksite facilities particularly safe drinking water, shed and first aid medical facility.

Khera and Nayak's study on women workers and perceptions of the MGNREGA enquired about the significance of MGNREGA in the lives of rural women[38]. There were variations in women's participation across the sampled areas. There were also issues of lack of crèche for mothers of young children and the continued illegal presence of contractors. Given the critical gains made by women workers- in accessing work and an income, food and healthcare for themselves and their families, and in leaving potentially hazardous work-it needs to be ensured that the problems in implementation do not derails the gains.

They further pointed out the potential of MGNREGA to have a wider impact (over time) on gender relations. MGNREGA employment can enhance women's economic independence by providing them access to cash earnings. Moreover, MGNREGA earnings can bring about a sense of equality fostered by earning, for the first time, the same wage as men.

Jean Drèze who led a team for survey of 10 randomly selected *gram panchayats* in Jhalawar has examined the effectiveness of the programme in the rural areas. He observed that despite the existence of areas of concern such as delays in payments of wages and non-payment of minimum wages the track record, particularly in employment generation, has been impressive. The survey found the trend of positive change also in the implementation of transparency safeguards, such as in the maintenance of job cards and the muster rolls. However, these achievements are threatened by "growing official hostility to social audits initiated by citizens' organization and even to their involvement in the mandatory social audits to be conducted by *gram sabhas*. This dispute has raised important questions about the process of social audit, the agency of different institutions, the modalities of release of information, and related matters," said Prof. Drèze[39]. (The Hindu, 2008)

Dutt et al. posed a question which reflects in their article entitled "Does India's Employment Guarantee Scheme Guarantee Employment?". An analysis of the NSS data for 2009-10 confirms expectations that poorer states of India have more demand for work under the MGNREGS. However, actual participation rates in the scheme are not (as a rule) any higher in poorer states where it is needed the most. The reason for this paradox lies in the differences in the extent to which the employment guarantee is honoured. The answer to the question posed in our title is clearly "no". Rationing is common, but far more so in some of the poorest states[40].

Hirway et.al.[41] conducted a study conducted in a village in Gujarat to examine the economic and gender equality implications of public job creation in economic activities currently served by unpaid work, including unpaid care work. The study argues that a well designed wage employment programme with a guarantee component, can not only address the immediate problem of ensuring employment and wages to the poor at the bottom, but can also contribute towards promoting pro-poor economic growth. The study builds a village level social accounting matrix (SAM) to estimate the employment, income and output multiplier impacts of MGNREGA works in a village in Gujarat. These multipliers tend to increase with time. MGNREGA works can also relieve women from the drudgery of unpaid work like collection of water, fuel, wood, fodder, material for shelther, craft, etc., by strengthening local infrastructure. The reduction in unpaid work can promote gender inequality as well as increase multiplier impacts through women's participation in MGNREGA. The study has identified an approach to maximize the values of the multipliers in the short and long runs. One needs to focus on the basis entitlements of MGNREGA that form the core of the Act.

MGNREGA was enacted with lot of hope and aspiration for the poor and the vulnerable. It is surprising to know that there are still various loopholes in this right based pro-poor policy. There are state wise differences in the implementation of the Act. Some states tell success stories while some are still unable to address the poor. The voices of the poor are still unheard in many poor states. The nature of work doesn't motivate people to improve their skills as it is not skill based. Following operational guidelines is not mandatory. As a result, state governments implement the act according to their convenience. There are many challenges in implementing the act. Unless and until, these loopholes are taken care of, poverty eradication will still remain a distant dream.

Endnotes

1 Government of India (2011) "Census of India, Office of the Registrar General and Census Commissioner"; Government of India.

2 Government of India (2007) "Eleventh Five Year Plan,Vol.I,II & III"; Planning Commission, Government of India.

3 Right to Food (2007) "Employment Guarantee Act: A Primer"; Right to Food Campaign Secretariat, New Delhi.

4 Government of India (2011) "Economic Survey of India 2010-11"; Ministry of Finance, Government of India, New Delhi.

5 The poverty line is Rs.356 monthly per capita consumption expenditure for rural areas and Rs.539 for urban areas.

6 Government of India (2006) "61st Round Report of National Sample Survey Organisation", July 2004-June 2005, Ministry of Statistics and Programme Implementation, Government of India, New Delhi.

7 United Nations Development Programme (2015) "Human Development Report 2015"; UNDP, .New York.

8 Government of India (1979) "Study of Crash Scheme for Rural Employment"; Programme Evaluation Organization(PEO),Study No.104, Planning Commission, Government of India, New Delhi.

9 Government of India (1973) "Report of the Committee on Unemployment (Bhagwati Committee)"; Government of India, New Delhi.

10 Government of India (1977) "Report of the Review Committee on Pilot Intensive Rural Employment Project (PIREP), Ministry of Irrigation and Agriculture, Government of India, New Delhi.

11 Government of India (1980) "Evaluation of Food for Work Programme"; Programme Evaluation Organization(PEO),Study No.114, Planning Commission, Government of India, New Delhi.

12 Government of India (1975) "Report on Evaluation Study of Small Farmers, Marginal Farmers and Agricultural Labourers Project, 1974-75; Chapter 6; Planning Commission, Government of India, New Delhi.

13 United Nations Development Programme (1993) "Human Development Report"; UNDP, New York.

14 Atul Kholi(1987) "The State and Poverty in India: The Politics of Reform"; Cambridge University Press, Cambridge.

15 Government of India (2002) "Tenth Five Year Plan,2002-07"; Vol.III;Planning Commission, Government of India,New Delhi.

16 Government of India(2000) " Evaluation of Study on Employment Assurance Scheme"; Programme Evaluation Organization(PEO), Planning Commission, Government of India, New Delhi

17 Government of India (2000) " Ninth Five Year Plan,2002-07"; Vol.II; Planning Commission, Government of India, New Delhi.

18 Indira Hirway, M.R. Saluja and Bhupesh Yadav (2010) "Employment Guarantee Programme and the Pro-Poor Growth: The study of a village in Gujarat"; Academic Foundation, New Delhi.

19 Government of India (2005) " The Gazette of India"; Extraordinary, Part II-Section 1,No.48;Ministry of Law and Justice, Government of India, New Delhi

20 Jean Drèze, and Christian Oldiges (2011) "MGNREGA:The Official Picture" in Reetika Khera ed. *The Battle for Employment Guarantee;* Oxford University Press, New Delhi. The same article was published as "Commendable Act" *Frontline,* 24 (14): 14-27,July 2007 and "Work in Progress", *Frontline,* 26 (4): 14-27,February2009.

21 Available at www.mgnrega.nic.in

22 Reetika Khera and Nandini Nayak(2009) "Women Workers and Perceptions of the National Rural Guarantee Act"; Economic and Political Weekly, Vol.XLIV No.43,October.

23 Puja Dutta, Rinku Murgai, Martin Ravallion and Dominique Van de Walle (2012) "Does India's Employment Guarantee Scheme Guarantee Employment?" Economic and Political Weekly, , 2012 Vol. XLVII No. 16, April pp. 55-64

24 Jayati Ghosh (2006) "The 'Right to Work' and Recent Legislation in India";Social Scientist, Vol.34.No.1/2 (Jan-Feb,2006), pp.88-102.

25 Pinaki Chakraborty (2007) "Implementation of Employment Guarantee: A Preliminary Appraisal"; Economic and Political Weekly, February 17,2007.pp.548-551.

26 Mihir Shah (2007) "Employment Guarantee, Civil Society and Indian Democracy" ; Economic and Political Weekly, Vol.XLII No.45-46,November 10,2007.

27 Santosh Mehrotra (2008) "NREG Two Years On: Where Do We Go From Here?"; *Economic and Political Weekly*; Vol.XLIII, No.31,August 02,2008.

28 Samarthan-Centre for Development Support(2006) "Status of MGNREGA Implementation: Grassroots Learning and Ways Forward"; 1st Monitoring Report. Available at http://www.empowerpoor.org/downloads/Statuspercent20ofpercent20MGNREGApercent20inpercent20PACSpercent20states.pdf.

29 Government of India (2007) "Performance Audit of Implementation of National Rural Employment Guarantee Act, 2005 (MGNREGA) draft report"; Comptroller and Auditor General, New Delhi.

30 Anupam Goswami (2008): "Jobs for the Poor"; Business India, Feb.10, 2008.

31 *Ibid.*

32 Anshuman Jaswal and Paulomee Mistry (2007) "Will MGNREGA Ensure Security Against Hunger?"; Disha. Available at: http://www.disha-india.org/Diwaspercent20Ugepercent20Nepercent20Dadipercent20Male.pdf

33 Institute of Applied Manpower Research (2007) "All India Report on Evaluation of MGNREGA: A Survey of Twenty Districts"; Programme Evaluation Organization (PEO), Planning Commission, Government of India.

34 Government of India (2006) "Unlocking Human Capital: Entitlements and Governance- A Case Study"; Second Administrative Commission Report. (Also available on http://arc.gov.in)

35 Government of India (2010) "Mahatma Gandhi National Rural Employment Guarantee Act, 2005(MGMGNREGA), Report to the People";Ministry of Rural Development, New Delhi. (Also available at www.MGNREGA.nic.in)

36 Rural Technology & Business Incubator (2009) "Evaluation of MGNREGA in Tamil Nadu"; Indian Institute of Technology, Madras.

37 National Federation of Indian Women (NIFW) (2008) "A Study on Socio-Economic Empowerment of Women under MGNREGA"; Ministry of Rural Development, Government of India.

38 Reetika Khera and Nandini Nayak(2009) "Women Workers and Perceptions of the National Rural Guarantee Act"; Economic and Political Weekly, Vol.XLIV No.43,October.

39 The Hindu (2008) "Despite hiccups, MGNREGA a boon for rural poor"; Sunday, Feb 10, 2008.

40 Puja Dutta, Rinku Murgai, Martin Ravallion and Dominique Van de Walle (2012) "Does India's Employment Guarantee Scheme Guarantee Employment?"; Economic and Political Weekly, 2012 Vol. XLVII No. 16, April .pp.55-64

41 Indira Hirway, M.R.Saluja and Bhupesh Yadav (2010) "Employment Guarantee Programme and Pro-Poor Growth; The Study of a Village in Gujarat"; Academic Foundation, New Delhi

3

Rajasthan-State Profile

Rajasthan, the fairy land of maharajas, palaces and tigers has a total area of 343,000 sq. km. It is the second largest state of India and is one of the few states that show a great contrast from one area to another. This disparity is noticeable in respect of climate, soil, vegetation, mineral resources etc. Rajasthan is an exotic state where tradition and glory meet in beautiful colours against the backdrop of sand and desert. It is also one of the driest regions in India. It is located in the northwest of India. It comprises most of the area of the large, inhospitable Great Indian Desert (Thar Desert), which parallels the Sutlej-Indus river valley along its border with Pakistan. The state is bordered by Pakistan to the west, Gujarat to the southwest, Madhya Pradesh to the southeast, Uttar Pradesh and Haryana to the northeast and Punjab to the north. Rajasthan covers 10.4 % of India, an area of 342,239 square kilometres (132,139 sq mi). Jaipur, known as the pink city is the capital and the largest city of the state.

Rajasthan is a melting pot of several races and the ethnic fabric of the state reflects a brilliant merger. Rajasthan of the yester years was a witness to the influence of the mighty *Rajputs*. Conjugal ties between feisty *Rajputs* and the powerful *Mughals* was fodder for an enviable lineage. The land of fortresses and golden hued sand is also home to several tribes like *Meenas, Bhils, Sahariyas, Sidhis, Gaduliya Lohars* and *Damors* among a host of others.

Rajasthan is culturally rich and has artistic and cultural traditions which reflect the ancient Indian way of life. There is rich and varied folk culture from villages which is often depicted and is symbolic of the state.

Figure 3.1: Map of Rajasthan

Source: www.mapsofindia.com

Highly cultivated classical music and dance with its own distinct style is part of the cultural tradition of Rajasthan. The music is uncomplicated and songs depict day-to-day relationships and chores, more often focused around fetching water from wells or ponds.

Geographical Profile

The most striking feature of this land is its division by the majestic Aravalli range which runs from north east to south-west for about 688 km. northwest of the Aravallis are the Jodhpur, Jaisalmer,

Barmer and Bikaner regions, it is the home of arid plains and the shifting sand dunes of the great Thar Desert. The other side of the hills is a land rich in vegetation – The Aravalli.

Mount Abu lies at the south western end of the range, separated from the main ranges by the West Banas River, although a series of broken ridges continues into Haryana in the direction of Delhi where it can be seen as outcrops in the form of the Raisina Hill and the ridges farther north. About three-fifths of Rajasthan lies northwest of the Aravallis, leaving two-fifths on the east and south direction.

In the west, Rajasthan is relatively dry and infertile; this area includes some of the Thar Desert, also known as the Great Indian Desert. In the south western part of the state, the land is wetter, hilly, and more fertile. The climate varies throughout Rajasthan. On average winter temperatures range from 8° to 28° C (46° to 82° F) and summer temperatures range from 25° to 46° C (77° to 115° F). Average rainfall also varies; the western deserts accumulate about 100 mm (about 4 in) annually, while the south eastern part of the state receives 650 mm (26 in) annually, most of which falls from July through September during the monsoon season.

Socio-Economic Profile

Rajasthan has mainly Rajasthani population. According to Census 2011, Hindus account for 88.8% of the population. Muslims make up 8.5%, Sikhs 1.4% and Jains 1.2% of the population. The state of Rajasthan is also populated by Sindhis, who came to Rajasthan from Sindh province (now in Pakistan) during the India-Pakistan separation in 1947[1].

The mother tongue of the majority of people in Rajasthan is Rajasthani. Rajasthani and Hindi are the most widely used languages in Rajasthan. Rajasthani is used as a medium of instruction, along with Hindi and English, in some schools. Some other languages used in Rajasthan are Gujarati, Sindhi and Punjabi.

The population of Rajasthan according to the 2011 census stands at about 68 million, making it the 8th most populated state in India. The state makes up about 5.6% of the country's population a figure which was about 5.4% during the last census in 2001. Of the total population of Rajasthan state, around 75.11 percent live in the villages of rural areas. In actual numbers, males and females were 26,680,882 and 24,859,354 respectively. Total population of rural areas of

Rajasthan state was 51,540,236. The population growth rate recorded for this decade (2001-2011) was 19.05%. Out of total population of Rajasthan, 24.89% people live in urban regions. The total figure of population living in urban areas is 17,080,776 of which 8,939,204 are males and while remaining 8,141,572 are females. The urban population in the last 10 years has increased by 29.26 percent.

Table 3.1: Demographic Profile of Rajasthan

Description	2011
Approximate Population	6.86 Crore
Actual Population	6,86,21,012
Rural	5,15,40,236
Urban	1,70,80,776
Male	3,56,20,086
Rural	2,66,80,882
Urban	89,39,204
Female	3,30,00,926
Rural	2,48,59,354
Urban	81,41,572
Population Growth (2001-11)	21.44%
Percentage of total Population	5.67%
Sex Ratio	926
Child Sex Ratio	67%
Density/km2	201
Literacy	67.06%
Male Literacy	80.51%
Female Literacy	52.66%
Total Literate	3,89,70,500
Male Literate	2,41,84,782
Female Literate	1,47,85,718

Source: Census 2011

The state has a growth rate of about 21% percent which is the

11th highest growth rate in the country. The population of the state is rising considerably due to rapid efforts towards development and progress. The literacy rate in the state is about 67% which is a cause for concern and a statistic the authorities must take notice of and look to correct in the years to come.

Sex ratio in Rajasthan is 926 i.e. for each 1000 male, which is below national average of 940 as per census 2011. In 2001, the sex ratio of female was 922 per 1000 males in Rajasthan. The sex ratio in Rajasthan also leaves a lot to be desired as it lags behind the national average by 10 points. The statistics in the Rajasthan census 2011 reveal facts that can be taken into consideration by the government in a bid to further its development. The state is spread over an area of about 340000 sq. km. making it the largest state in the country in terms of area. The density of population per sq. km. is about 201 and below the national average.

Literacy rate in Rajasthan has seen upward trend and is 67.06 percent as per 2011 population census. Of that, male literacy stands at 80.51 percent while female literacy is at 52.66 percent. In 2001, literacy rate in Rajasthan stood at 60.41 percent of which male and female were 70.32 percent and 43.85 percent literate respectively. In actual numbers, total literates in Rajasthan stands at 38,970,500 of which males were 24,184,782 and females were 14,785,718.

In Rajasthan, the main proportion of rural population is of the Other Backward Class (OBC). There is also a fair percentage of Scheduled Tribe (SC) population. The main proportion of urban population is dominated by others which are not in the underprivileged class. The Scheduled Tribe population in urban area is very low (2.5 percent) as compared to other classes.

Table 3.2 :Percentage Distribution of Population by Social Group in Rajasthan[2]

S.C.	S.T.	OBC	Others	All
Rural				
20.9	16.0	46.6	16.3	100
Urban				
20.8	2.5	37.6	38.9	100

Source: NSS 61st Round

Rajasthan's economy is predominantly agrarian in nature and there are wide fluctuations in the agricultural production which is dependent on rainfall. The growth rate of Gross State Domestic Product is fluctuating and this can be attributed largely to the uncertainties in the agricultural production in the State. In simple terms, the Gross State Domestic Product (GSDP) is the total monetary value of all the final goods and services produced by an economy during a given period of time (generally a year) accounted without duplication. The estimates of Gross and Net State Domestic Product (GSDP & NSDP) and Per-Capita Income (PCI) have been prepared both at current and constant (2004-05) prices. The year-wise estimates of Gross & Net State Domestic Product and Per-Capita Income from the year 2007-08 at current prices are given below[3]:

Table 3.3: Gross & Net State Domestic Product and Per-Capita Income from the Year 2007-08 at Current Prices

Year	At Current Prices		
	GSDP (₹Crore)	NSDP(₹Crore)	PCI(₹)
2007-08	1,94,822	1,72,250	26,882
2008-09	2,30,949	2,03,939	31,279
2009-10 P	2,63,258	2,31,963	34,982
2010-11 Q	3,23,682	2,86,008	42,434
2011-12 A	3,68,320	3,25,266	47,506

P-Provisional, Q-Quick, A-Advance
Source: Government of Rajasthan

The year-wise estimates of Gross & Net State Domestic Product and Per Capita Income from the year 2007-08 at constant (2004-05) prices are given below:

Table 3.4: Gross & Net State Domestic Product and Per Capita Income from the Year 2007-08 at Constant (2004-05) Prices

Year	At Constant(2004-05) Prices		
	GSDP (₹Crore)	NSDP (₹Crore)	PCI(₹)
2007-08	1,60,017	1,40,471	21,922
2008-09	1,74,556	1,52,284	23,356
2009-10 P	1,84,189	1,60,248	24,166
2010-11 Q	2,04,398	1,78,184	26,436
2011-12 A	2,15,454	1,87,749	27,421

P-Provisional, Q-Quick, A-Advance
Source: Government of Rajasthan

The advance estimates of Gross State Domestic Product at current prices is estimated to be Rs.3,68,320 crore for the year 2011-12 as compared to Rs. 3,23,682 crore during the year 2010-11 (quick estimates), showing an increase of 13.79 per cent over the previous year. As per the advance estimates, Gross State Domestic Product at constant (2004-05) prices, in the year 2011-12 is likely to attain a level of Rs.2,15,454 crore, as against the estimates of GSDP for the year 2010-11 (quick estimates) of Rs.2,04,398 crore, registering an increase of 5.41 per cent over the preceding year.

The advance estimates of Net State Domestic Product at current prices is worked out to be Rs.3,25,266 crore for the year 2011-12 as compared to Rs.2,86,008 crore during the year 2010-11 (quick estimates) showing an increase of 13.73 per cent over the previous year. As per the advance estimates, the Net State Domestic Product at constant (2004-05) prices, in the year 2011-12 has been estimated at Rs.1, 87,749 crore as against Rs.1, 78,184 crore in the year 2010-11 (quick estimates) showing an increase of 5.37 per cent over the previous year.

The per capita income for the year 2011-12 at current prices works out to be Rs.47, 506 as against Rs. 42,434 during the year 2010-11 registering an increase of 11.95 per cent over the previous year. The per capita income at 2004-05 constant prices during 2011-12, is likely to be Rs.27, 421 as compared to Rs.26, 436 in the year 2010-11, registering an increase of 3.73 per cent over the previous year.

The increase in labour force bears a direct co-relation to the increase in the population. As per 1981 census, 36.6 percent of the total population were working. In 2001, there is an increase of 5.5 percent. However it is interesting to note that the work participation rate among the males is decreasing and female work participation rate is increasing.

Table 3.5 : Work Participation Rate in Rajasthan from 1981-2001 (in percent)

Year	Total Workers			Main Workers			Marginal Workers		
	1981	1991	2001	1981	1991	2001	1981	1991	2001
Persons	36.6	38.5	42.1	30.4	31.5	30.8	6.13	6.95	11.2
Males	50.9	49.07	33.5	49.9	48.2	43.6	0.98	0.81	6.3
Females	21.06	27.01	50	9.3	13.3	16.9	11.74	13.67	16.5

Source: Census 1981, 1991, 2001

The main workers among the male is decreasing and vice versa in the case of female workers. This indicates that female work participation is increasing over the years. It is a positive indication that the female counterpart is also actively involved as workers. Similarly the marginal workers in all the categories have also increased over the last three decades.

According to the Census, 2011, Rajasthan is divided in to thirty three districts and two hundred and forty nine blocks for administrative purpose. The thirty three districts are divided into seven divisions. They are:

- Ajmer Division: Ajmer, Bhilwara, Nagaur, Tonk.
- Bharatpur Division: Bharatpur, Dholpur, Karauli, Sawai Madhopur.
- Bikaner Division: Bikaner, Churu, Sri Ganganagar, Hanumangarh.
- Jaipur Division: Jaipur, Alwar, Jhunjhunu, Sikar, Dausa.
- Jodhpur Division: Barmer, Jaisalmer, Jalore, Jodhpur, Pali, Sirohi.
- Kota Division: Baran, Bundi, Jhalawar, Kota.
- Udaipur

The districts are further divided as tribal districts (7 districts), desert districts (6 districts) and plain districts (20 districts).The total revenue villages are forty four thousand six hundred seventy two.

Rajasthan and MGNREGA

The State Government of Rajasthan in line with the MGNREGA has formulated its own scheme titled Rajasthan Rural Employment Guarantee Scheme (RREGS).The RREGS was implemented in six districts namely Banswara, Dungarpur, Jhalawar, Karauli, Sirohi and Udaipur in the first phase. By 2009, all the districts were covered under the RREGS. The performance of Rajasthan in the implementation of MGNREGA in the initial phase has been impressive. It was considered to be one of the best performing states in India. When the Act was enacted, Rajasthan was already prepared for its implementation. The fact lies that Rajasthan has played an active role in the struggle for employment guarantee. The presence of civil society organisations gave further impetus to spread awareness about the Act. Rajasthan also has a long tradition of public mobilization for employment and wages in the context of drought relief. When MGNREGA came into force, it was quickly recognised as a crucial opportunity for the rural poor. Public interest in the Act quickly translated into serious pressure on the state government to act.[4]

Endnotes

1 Government of India (2011) "Census of India, Office of the Registrar General and Census Commissioner"; Government of India.

2 Government of India (2006) "61st Round Report of National Sample Survey Organisation", July 2004-June 2005, Ministry of Statistics and Programme Implementation, Government of India, New Delhi.

3 Government of Rajasthan (2012) "Economic Review 2011-12"; Planning Department, Directorate of Economics and Statistics, Rajasthan.

4 Jean Drèze and Reetika Khera (2009) "The Battle for Employment Guarantee"; Frontline, 26 (1): 3-16,January 2009.

4

Implementation of MGNREGA in Rajasthan

Public policy implementation is one of the most crucial stages in the policy process. Policy implementation is the action part of the process. The fate of a policy is decided by the way it is implemented. Policy scientists assumed that once a policy is formulated, it will be implemented. But the big question is whether the objectives of the policy will be achieved or not? It has been observed that there is a gap between the formulation and implementation of public policies.

MGNREGA has placed judicially enforceable obligations on the state to provide 100 days of guaranteed employment to every rural household. This is a right based approach which guarantees right to work to every rural household whose adult members are willing to do unskilled manual work. Some of the important provisions of the Act are discussed below which are meant for an effective implementation of the Act. The fact remains that whatever the critics say about the policy, the policy is benefiting the poor particularly the deprived sections of the societies. It has also played a positive role among the women of the rural areas. The most significant aspect in MGNREGA is its right based approach which led to a major decline in the exploitation of poor households. This chapter will look at the implementation of MGNREGA in Dungarpur, Jhalawar, Sirohi and Udaipur.

Dungarpur

Dungarpur district of Rajasthan is situated in the southern most part of Rajasthan 23.200 to 24.010 of latitude and 73.210 to 74.230 of longitude. In East and North it borders on Banswara and Udaipur districts respectively while it adjoins the state of Gujarat in South and West. It is the smallest district of the state covering 3,771 sq. km. only which is 2.02 percent of the total area of Rajasthan.

Figure 4.1: Map of Dungarpur

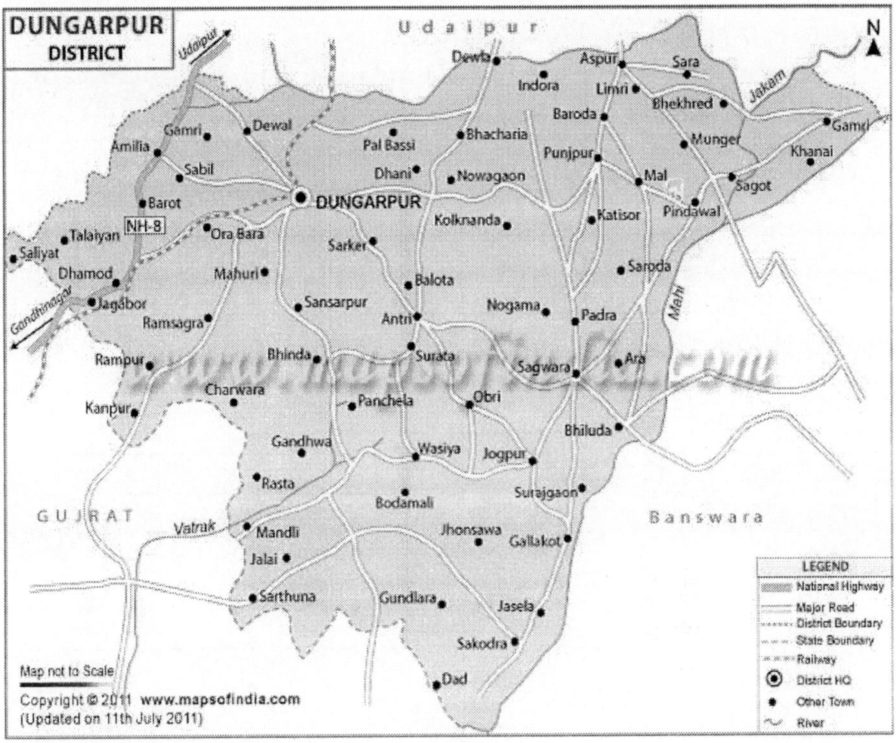

Source: www.mapsofindia.com

The district Dungarpur is named after "the town of hillocks" and the capital of the former princely state of Dungarpur. The town of Dungarpur itself is said to have been a Bhil[1] Pal or a hamlet of Dungaria, a Bhil chieftain. It is believed that Rawal Veer Singh Dev assassinated Dungaria and founded Dungarpur in the fourteenth century. Dungarpur, once, used to be a major territory of the Vagad region with Vatpadrak, present Baroda (a village in Aspur tehsil) as its old capital.

Dungarpur is mainly a hilly region so it also called the "City of Hills". The terrain of Dungarpur is interspersed with stony hills covered with a jungle of cactus, jojoba trees and *salar* (a gum producing tree), together with several other varieties of shrubs and trees not requiring deep soil or moisture. This terrain is not typically an agricultural area, since a large part of the district here consists of hills, valleys and rocky surfaces. While some lands permit normal sedentary agriculture, in large parts crops are grown on hilly and undulating slopes, yielding low crop yields.

District Profile of Dungarpur

According to Census 2001, Dungarpur had a population of 11, 07,643 of which males were 547,791 and remaining 559,852 were females. In 2011, the population of Dungarpur increased to 13, 88,906. Out of the total population, the male population is 698,069 and the female population is 690,837. The district population in 2011 constituted 2.02 percent of total Rajasthan population. As per 2001 census, it was at 1.96 percent of Rajasthan population. The provisional data of the Census, 2011 reveals that density of Dungarpur district is 368 people per sq.km. In 2001, the density was at 294 people per sq.km.

Table 4.1 : Demographic Profile of Dungarpur District

Description	2011	2001
Population	**13,88,906**	**11,07,643**
Male	6,98,069	5,47,791
Female	6,90,837	5,59,852
Population Growth	**25.39%**	**22.46%**
Area Sq. Km	3,771	3,771
Density/km2	**368**	**294**
Proportion to Rajasthan Population	2.02%	1.96%
Average Literacy (%)	**60.78**	**48.57**
Male Literacy	74.66	66.04
Female Literacy	46.98	31.77
Rural-Urban Population in 2011	**Rural**	**Urban**
Population (%)	93.61%	6.39%
Total Population	**13,00,129**	**88,777**
Male Population	6,52,478	45,591
Female Population	6,47,651	43,186

Source: Census of India

The average literacy rate of Dungarpur in 2011 is 60.78 per cent which has increased from 48.57 per cent in 2001. The male and female literacy rate in 2001 was 66.04 percent and 31.77 per cent.

The literacy rate among male and female also increased in 2011 to 74.66 and 46.98 respectively.

In 2011, 93.61 per cent of population of Dungarpur district lives in rural areas of villages. Out of 13, 00,129 of the total rural population of Dungarpur, 652,478 are male and 647,651 are female population. The urban population in 2011 is 6.39 per cent. In total 88,777 people live in urban areas of which 45,591 are males and 43,186 are females.

This is a predominantly rural, agricultural district. There are 872 revenue villages (237 gram *panchayats*) and only two towns and hence, this density could be termed as rather high. The labour participation ratio was 47 per cent which includes 51.3 per cent for male and 44.7 per cent for female, as per the census of 2001. The proportion engaged in agriculture (cultivators plus agricultural labourers) was about 76 per cent. Women formed 53.3 per cent of the agricultural work force. The work participation ratio is much higher in the district compared to the state average, principally due to a larger female participation ratio, a feature noted in most (*Bhil*) tribal regions.

The district has a high concentration of people belonging to the ST groups. The average (including rural and urban areas) was 65 per cent as per the 2001 census. The highest concentration is in the south (i.e. the *tehsils* of Sagwara and Simalwara). However, social structure of the population appears to be changing since 1981. The decadal growth rate of the non-SC/ST population observes an increase from below 20 per cent during 1961-71 to over 32 per cent during 1991-2001. The SC/ST population, predominantly ST population, on the other hand register a decline in growth rate; from 38 per cent to 25 per cent during the same period (Figure 4.2)[2].

Figure 4.2: Changing Social Structure of Population-Decadal Growth Rates of Population by Social Groups in Dungarpur

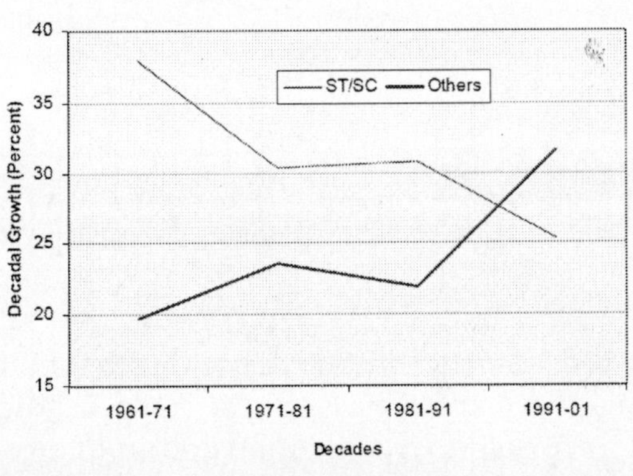

The proportion of ST labour population to total agricultural labour population in rural areas was recorded at about 77 percent (in 2001) which is higher than their proportion in the population. Implicitly, ST population is poorer than the rest casual as casual labourers are among the economically weakest sections in the Indian society.

Implementation of MGNREGA in Dungarpur

When the Act was launched in February, 2006, Dungarpur was one the districts where MGNREGA was implemented in the first phase. One of the main reasons for choosing Dungarpur in the initial phase was that it falls in the poor tribal belt of southern Rajasthan where heavy labour out-migration occurs every year. It has also been identified as one of the backward districts of the country.[3] It is also a compact district, manageable for such an initiative.

The two blocks which were selected using purposive sampling technique are Asspur and Bicchiwada. As has been discussed earlier, one *gram panchayat* in each block has been selected using snowball sampling method. In Asspur, *Gol Panchayat* and in Bicchiwada block, Bicchiwada *panchayat* has been selected.

Figure 4.3: Sample of Dungarpur District

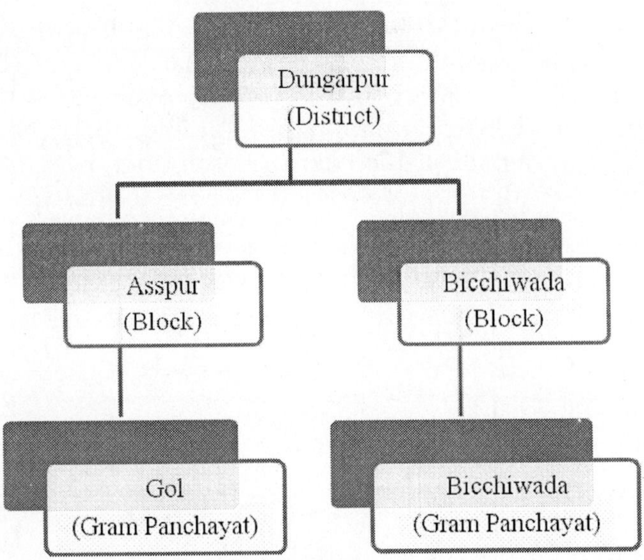

In each *gram panchayat*, 30 respondents who are beneficiaries of the scheme were interviewed. In Asspur, the interview was conducted at a worksite where construction of a road was going on in the interior of Danela village. According to the Bicchiwada *panchayat* members, there was no work going on at the time of the visit for data collection. Since there was no work going on, the villagers were interviewed in a school which was being used by the *panchayat* members during vacation of the school. The total people interviewed in Dungarpur block is sixty. The data collected from the beneficiaries will be analysed using Statistical Package for the Social Science (SPSS)[4].It is a software package used for statistical analysis of data. The data analysis will be confined to cross tabulation and frequencies of descriptive statistics.

This district has the privilege of having at least two membership based organizations such as the Vagad Mazdoor Kisan Sanghathan(VMKS),a partner of the Mazdoor Kisan Shakti Sanghatan (MKSS) and Dakshini Rajasthan Mazdoor Union (DRMU).These organization undertook door-to-door campaigns telling people about the provisions of the National Rural Employment Guarantee Act and the rights and entitlements of the people which resulted in the end of starvation, a reduction in the migration and providing employment to more than 1.5 lakh laborers.

Sample Respondents

In both the *gram panchayat* i.e. Gol and Bicchiwada, the sampled workers were from Scheduled Tribe (ST) category. The work force from general caste category does not work under MGNREGA. They consider that their social status does not permit to work under MGNREGA which is meant for marginalized sections of the society. The caste bias is vividly visible among the villagers.

Table 4.2 : Sample Respondents in Dungarpur

Caste	Male	Female	Total
		Gol	
ST	11 (36.7)	19(63.3)	30(100)
		Bicchiwada	
ST	6(20)	24(80)	30(100)

Figures in brackets indicates percentage

The above table gives a glimpse of the sample workers who have been interviewed. The proportion of male respondents in both the *gram panchayat* is 36.7 percent in Gol *panchayat* and 20 percent in Bicchiwada *panchayat* respectively. The proportion of female participation is more than male in both the *gram panchayat*. In Gol *panchayat* the female participation is 63.3 percent and 80 percent of the workers in Bicchiwada is female. Rajasthan has been one of the states in India with a large percentage of women work participation. As per the Ministry of Rural Development, the work participation rate of women in December, 2012 is 69.2 percent. One of the reasons of large percentage of women work participation rate is that their male counterpart prefers to continue with their respective occupations. The wage rate of MGNREGA is lower as compared to what they get from their work. According to the *panchayat* members, men do not want to work for a low wage rate. The self-esteem of men hurts to work for a mere sum. Moreover, the work provided under MGNREGA is for a limited time period.

One of the positive impacts of MGNREGA is that it has helped women in rural areas to come out of their closed shell. The women respondents said that the enactment of MGNREGA has been a fortunate thing to them. The wage from MGNREGA income is an additional income for the family. It has a social impact as well in the lives of women. In rural areas, mostly women are treated as subordinate in a household. They do not have a say in the family. However, after MGNREGA it has changed their social status. They are also taking active part in the decision making of the family.

Household Size

'Household' will mean a nuclear family comprising mother, father, and their children, and may include any person wholly or substantially dependent on the head of the family. Household will also mean a single-member family. The work under MGNREGA is provided to those households whose adult members are willing to work as unskilled labour. The work is provided for 100 days in a financial year to every household.

The average family size in Gol *panchayat* is 5-6. In Bicchwada, the average size of household is less compared to Gol which is 3-4. Households with fewer members are more benefitted by the Act as compared to those with a large family. Many of the respondents have complained that this criterion is unfair to those with large families. The income of a single household with large number of members is not sufficient for the entire family. According to the *panchayat* members of both the *gram panchayats,* in families with large household there is a tendency among the children to separate their aged parents and get them registered as separate households. This becomes difficult for the *panchayats* to identify the households. Since MGNREGA work is demand driven, the demand for work also increases manifold. It becomes difficult for them to create enough work for the households.

Table 4.3: Household Size of Respondents in Dungarpur

No. of Household members	Frequency	Percent	Cumulative Percent
Gol			
1-2	2	6.7	6.7
3-4	5	16.7	23.3
5-6	15	50	73.3
7-8	7	23.3	96.7
9-10	1	3.3	100
Total	30	100	
Bicchiwada			
1-2	6	20	20
3-4	12	40	60
5-6	10	33.3	93.3
7-8	2	6.7	100
Total	30	100	

Figures in brackets indicates percentage

Profile of the Sample Respondents

The background of the workers has been discussed in the following table. This will give an idea about their economic condition. It can help in assessing the impact of the policy in the lives of the people.

Table 4.4 : Profile of Sample Respondent in Dungarpur

Household Income(Monthly)	BPL card holder	Land Holding			Total
		Landless	1-5 Bigha	6-10 Bigha	
Gol					
Only MGNREGA wage	No	4(3.3)	10(33.3)	0	14(46.7)
1000-1500	No	0	9(63.3)	1(3.3)	10(33.3)
1500-2000	No	1(3.3)	3(10.0)	1(3.3)	5(16.7)
2000-2500	No	0	1(3.3)	0	1(3.3)
Total		5(16.7)	23(76.6)	2(6.7)	30(100)
Bicchiwada					
1000-1500	Yes	2(6.7)	21(70)	0	23(76.6)
1500-2000	Yes	0	3(10.0)	0	3(10.0)
2000-2500	Yes	0	3(10.0)	0	3(10.0)
4000 & above	Yes	0	1(3.3)	0	1(3.3)
Total		2(6.7)	28(93.3)	0	30(100)

Figures in brackets indicates percentage

In Gol *panchayat* none of the respondents have a BPL card whereas in Bicchiwada *panchayat* it's the other way round. When we look at Table 3.4, it shows that the monthly household income as well as land holding in Gol is very low. Out of the total respondent of 30 in Gol, 46.7 percent are dependent completely on MGNREGA wage. In Gol, 16.7 percent of the total respondents are landless and 13.3 per cent landless households are entirely dependent on MGNREGA wage. Despite that the household members do not have a Below Poverty Line (BPL) card. It shows that the identification of poor households need to be strengthened. Most of the respondents have been fighting to get themselves enrolled under the BPL category. The villagers also complained that they have been requesting to provide them with a BPL card. The *Sarpanch* have been trying to get the villagers enrolled for BPL category but unable to do so. Despite his effort of pressurization on the higher authority, the officials are not taking any action.

As compared to Gol *panchayat,* the condition of workers is better in Bicchiwada. All the respondents are BPL card holders which enable them to avail benefits of government schemes for poor households.

The average income in Bicchiwada is Rs.1000-1500 per month. Only one person out of 30 has a monthly income of Rs. 4000 and above. Most of the respondents i.e. 93.3 percent have land holdings of 1-5 Bigha.

Awareness Level

While implementing a policy it is essential that the targeted population is aware about the policy. Unless and until the targeted population does not participate, the policy cannot be implemented effectively. So, spreading awareness regarding the policy is also an important part in the implementation of a policy. The people of Rajasthan were well aware about MGNREGA which they commonly called Narega or Job Card. But it was found that they were not aware about the provisions of the Act.

Table 4.5: Awareness Among the Respondents About the Provisions of the Act in Dungarpur

Educational Qualification	Gram Sabha Held				Source of Information about the Act		Signed Receipt after applying for Job		Unemployment Allowance	
	Yes	Yes (only Panchayat members)	No	No Idea	Villagers	Panchayat members	Yes	No	Yes	No
Gol										
Illiterate	10 (33.3)	0	11 (36.7)	9 (30.0)	11 (36.7)	19 (63.3)	0	30 (100)	0	30 (100)
Total	10 (33.3)	0	11 (36.7)	9 (30.0)	11 (36.7)	19 (63.3)	0	30 (100)	0	30 (100)
Bicchiwada										
Illiterate	6 (20.0)	0	11 (36.7)	12 (40.0)	12 (40.0)	17 (56.6)	5 (16.7)	24 (80.0)	0	29 (96.6)
VI-VIII	0	0	1 (3.3)	0	0	1 (3.3)	0	1 (3.3)	0	1 (3.3)
Total	6 (20.0)	0	12 (40.0)	12 (40.0)	12 (40.0)	18 (60.0)	5 (16.7)	25 (83.3)	0	30 (100)

Figures in brackets indicates percentage

All the respondents in Gol were illiterate and they also do not send their children to school. According to them, the school has been just established and there are inadequate teachers. Only 33.3 percent were aware about *gram sabhas* held for MGNREGA. The *sarpanch* of Dhanela village under Gol *panchayat* said that *gram sabha* for MGNREGA are held every three months. But, 36.7 percent of the respondents said that no *gram sabha* was held and 30 percent were unaware whether *gram sabha* was held or not. Majority of the workers got the information about MGNREGA schemes from the Panchayat members. None of them get a signed receipt after applying for a job. Since most of them are illiterate they do not apply for job. They verbally request the *panchayat* members to provide them work. If a worker who has applied for work under MGNREGA is not provided employment within 15 days from the date on which work is requested, an unemployment allowance shall be payable by the State Government at the rate prescribed in the Act. However, not a single person was aware about unemployment allowance. Nor the *panchayat* members gave the information on the detailed provisions of the Act.

In terms of awareness about the details of the Act, the stipulation in Bicchiwada is also more or less same. Only 20 percent said that *gram sabha* was held in Bicchiwada while 40 per cent had no clue on *gram sabha* in the village. During interview *panchayat* members said that *gram sabha* are held every two months but the villagers barely attend. To spread the news regarding *gram sabhas,* they distribute pamphlets in the villages. When applied for a job, only 16.7 percent got a signed receipt of their application for job. As in the case of Gol *panchayat,* here also none of the workers were aware of the unemployment allowances. Unless and until the beneficiaries are aware about their rights the implementation of the Act will remain incomplete. The reason for their lack of knowledge is the fact that they are illiterate. Moreover, the *panchayat* members do not provide them the detailed information regarding their rights under the Act. The respondents said that "the *panchayats* are the decision making body and whatever they decide is satisfactory for us". They have total confidence on the *panchayats.* The *panchayat* members need to play a responsible and proactive role in order to spread awareness among the villagers.

Lack of awareness among the beneficiaries is one of the pertinent issues since the implementation of the Act started. Many studies have revealed that workers were unaware of their entitlement to 100 days of work in a financial year, about the minimum wage or of their right to being paid within fifteen days and their entitlement to unemployment allowance if they are not provided work within the stipulated time of fifteen days.

Duration of Getting a Job Card and Job After Applying

A Job Card (JC) is an identification which entitles a household to apply for job under NREG schemes. After due verification by the *gram panchayat,* JC should be provided within 15 days. Once a JC is issued, the household can apply for employment for 100 days. A written application seeking work is to be made to the GP or Block Office, stating the time and duration for which work is sought. The GP will issue a dated receipt of the written application for employment, against which the guarantee of providing employment within 15 days.

Table 4.6: Duration of Getting Job Card(JC) and Job After Applying in Dungarpur

Days	Gol		Bicchiwada	
	Duration of getting JC	On Demand-Job Duration	Duration of getting JC	On Demand-Job Duration
10-15 days	0	0	6(20)	0
15-20 days	4(13.3)	5(16.7)	0	0
20-25 days	1(3.3)	1(3.3)	0	1(3.3)
30 & above	25(83.3)	24(80)	24(80)	29(96.7)
Total	30(100)	30(100)	30(100)	30(100)

Figures in brackets indicates percentage

83.3 percent in Gol *panchayat* got a JC after a month and above. Similarly, on demand job was provided to most of the workers after a month and more. This shows that there is lack of efficiency in the delivery of the policy.

The case is not different in Bicchiwada where 80 percent got a JC after a month and above. A whopping 96.7 percent of the total respondents got a job on demand after a month and above. The essence of the Act lies in the fact that it is a demand driven approach. But the delay in providing job on demand is withering the significance of the pro poor policy. The *Panchayat* members revealed that no work have been provided since June-July, 2011. After six years of implementation of the policy, creating enough work has become a problem. There is less work left and the demand for work is increasing.

Number of Days Worked by the respondents in the Financial Year 2010-11

Under MGNREGA a household should be provided 100 days of guaranteed employment in a financial year. Work should be provided as and when demanded by any member of the household registered in the JC.

Figure 4.4: No of Days Worked by the Respondents in 2010-11 in Dungarpur

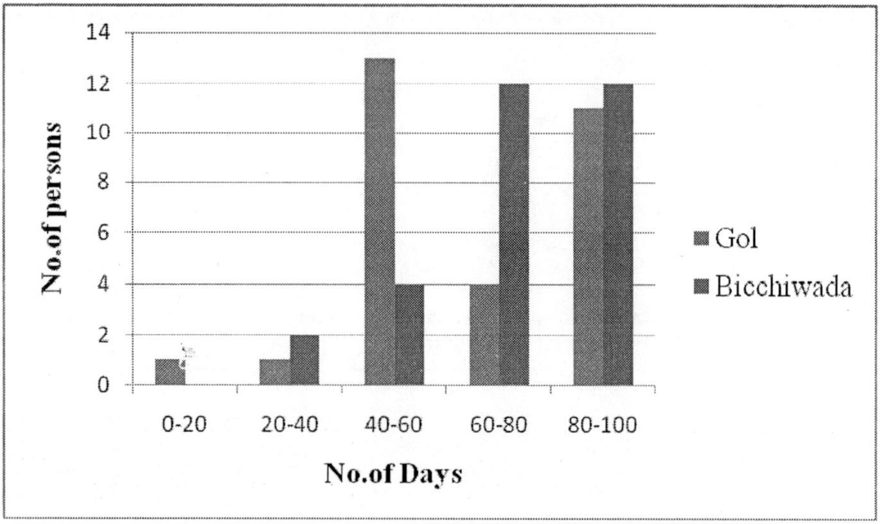

The field data reveals not many of the workers who are willing to work for 100 days are provided work on demand. We can see from the above figure that in Gol none of the respondents have completed 100 days of work. On an average,the respondents have worked in 2010-11 for only 40 days.

In Bicchiwada the scenario is better than Gol. Here, atleast 12 out of 30 have completed 100 days of work in the financial year 2010-11. The average day of working is double than Gol with 80 days of work in a year.

The basic entitlement of the Act is to provide 100 days of work. The findings from the field show that workers are willing to work for more than 100 days. The issue is lack of work to meet the demand of the job seeker.The PRI are unable to generate work for the people. The capacity of the PRI functionaries need to be stregthened. It was also found that PRI functionaries are not trained properly which is one of the reasons for their incapacities.

Payment Related Issues

Wages are to be paid as per the State-wise Government of India (GoI) notified MGNREGA wages. It has to be paid according to piece rate, as per the Schedule of Rates[1] (SoRs). Payment of wages has to be done on a weekly basis and not beyond a fortnight in any case. Payment of wages is mandatorily done through the individual/joint bank/post office beneficiary accounts[2]. The issue of late payment and none payment of stipulated wage has been of great concern in the implementation of the Act. The basic entitlements of the beneficiaries have not reached them.

Table 4.7: Payment Related Issues in Dungarpur

Gram Panchayat	Gol	Bicchiwada
Payment received per day(in Rs.)		
60-70	30(100)	0
70-80	0	2(6.7)
80-90	0	3(10.0)
90-100	0	11(36.7)
100 & above	0	14(46.7)
Total	30(100)	30(100)
Frequency of Payment		
15 days-1 month	7(23.3)	4(13.3)
1-2 months	13(43.3)	20(66.7)
2-3 months	10(33.3)	6(20.0)
Total	30(100)	30(100)

Figures in brackets indicates percentage

In Gol, the wage rate ranges between Rs.60-70. The wage is provided on the basis of work done in a day and not on attendance alone. The wage rate in Bicchiwada is higher than Gol. In Bicchiwada, 46.7 percent of the workers get more than Rs.100 in a day. But the positive aspect is that both men and women are paid equal wages.

Delay in payment has been a common phenomenon in both the *gram panchayat*. People complained that they are not paid on time. This is one of the reasons that many household are not entirely dependent on MGNREGA. The payments are made through bank account. The problem which crops up is that the workers have to go to the city where the banks are located to check for their payment. In rural areas commutation is difficult and after travelling a long distance, the workers get disappointed when they don't get their payment. Another issue which is quite pertinent is the issue of opening bank accounts. Many a time, the workers do not have identity and address proof for opening bank account. The bank does not open their account which is a hindrance to their access to work.

Worksite Related Issues

While allocating work, Work is to be provided within 5 km radius of the village. In case, work is provided beyond 5 km, extra wages of 10 per cent are payable to meet additional transportation and living expenses.

Table 4.8: Worksite Related Issues in Dungarpur

Gram Panchayats	Gol	Bicchiwada
Distance of worksite(in kms)		
1 km	5(16.7)	3(10.0)
2 km	7(23.3)	4(13.3)
3 km	9(30.0)	6(20.0)
4 km	3(10.0)	9(30.0)
5 km	4(13.3)	7(23.3)
6 km	2(6.7)	1(3.3)
Total	30(100)	30(100)
Worksite Facilities		
Nothing	9(30.0)	10(33.3)
Shade	7(23.3)	8(26.7)
Water and Tent	1(3.3)	0
Water	10(33.3)	7(23.3)
Water and Shade	3(10.0)	5(16.7)
Total	30(100)	30(100)

Figures in brackets indicates percentage

In Gol, 30 percent of the total workers come from 3 km. Only two, out of 30 comes from a distance of 6 km. The worksite facilities in Gol *panchayat* are found to be poor. 33.3 percent of the workers said that they are provided with water and 30.0 percent revealed that there is no worksite facilities provided. They also complained that they have to carry their own tools for working. They said that other than worksite facilities they should be provided with working tools. It has been observed that there was no worksite facility provided at the worksite in Dhanela village.

Most of the workers in Bicchiwada come from a distance of 4 km. Works are usually provided within the vicinity of the village. In Bicchiwada, 33.3 percent responded that no worksite facilities were provided. About 26 percent said that they are provided shade during summer at the worksite and 23.3 percent told that they are provided water.

Medical aid, drinking water, shade, and crèche if there are more than five children below the age of six years will have to be provided (MGNREGA, Schedule II, Sections 27 and 28). The maximum work force is women in both the *gram panchayat*. However, there is no crèche facility for their children. They have to leave their younger children with elder children. It has also been found that there was no medical aid at the worksite.

Overall Observation

The implementation in Bicchiwada is more systematic and efficient as compared to Gol *panchayat*. At the time of visit in Bicchiwada, no work was carried out. The interview with the beneficiaries revealed that they are satisfied with the functioning of the panchayat members. They are committed and work for the progress of their village. The interview with *panchayat* members show that the delay in approval by the officials led to delay in providing work and payments. Both the BDOs of Asspur and Bicchiwada were not available for interview during the visit.

It was observed that the impact of MGNREGA on the lives of the people has been positive in both the *gram panchayats*. For landless labour, the wage from MGNREGA is of great help. For others the income from MGNREGA helps them to get their basic necessity fulfilled. The policy also has a significant impact on the lives of women. They are now more empowered and they feel that they are now worth in the family.

There are grey areas in the implementation of the policies. One of the main objectives of the Act was to check migration. However it has been found that migration in the area still continues. The only change is that earlier it was the whole family household who used to migrate but now only the male or earning members of the household continue to work outside the district and state.

Picture 4.1: Women Workers in Asspur Block.

The girl with black stole (*dupatta*) is Maya Kanuji of Gol Panchayat in Asspur block. She is only 16 years old and an orphan. She has to take care of her two siblings'; one younger brother and one younger sister. She is not eligible to work under MGNREGA because she is not an adult. The *Pradhan* has provided her work under MGNREGA looking at her circumstances. Despite the fact that it is sheer violation of the Act that she is employed but for Maya MGNREGA is the only means of livelihood in rural area. With the earnings from MGNREGA work, she sends her younger brother to school that is in seventh grade. For some people like Maya, MGNREGA is a boon.

Jhalawar

Jhalawar lies in the south-eastern region of Rajasthan, at the edge of Malwa Plateau. The region, known for richness in forests, has exotic flora and fauna and is a heaven for numerous species of birds which can be spotted on the roads as one drives along the lush-green fields.

Jhalawar is situated in the south-eastern part of Rajasthan with an area of about 6322 Sq.km. It resembles the letter 'S' and lies between 23.45° and 24.52° N and between 75.27° and 76.56° E. It is bounded on the south-east by the state of Madhya Pradesh and on the north-west by Baran district and Kota district.

Figure 4.5: Map of Jhalawar

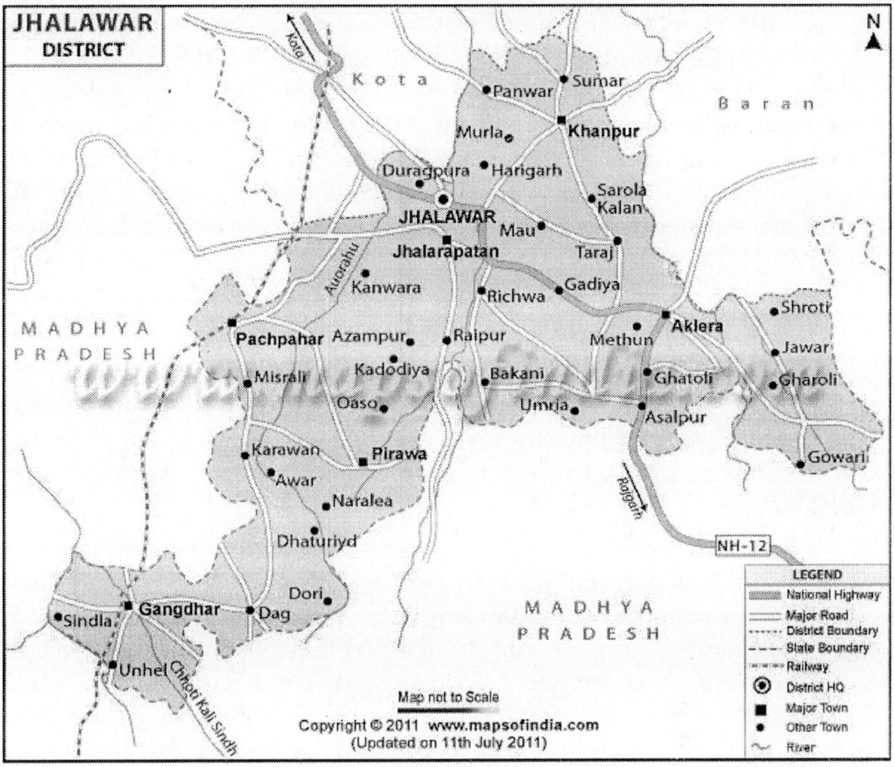

Source: www.mapsofindia.com

Jhalawar was a part of Malwa Pradesh during the Mughal period. Jhalawar was given to Raghav Jhala in Jagir by the ruler of Mandu in the year 1420 A.D. Since then the region is known as Jhalawar or the land of Jhalas. The princely state of Jhalawar was created in 1838 A. D. after being separated from Kota by the British. It got its name derived from Jhalas, a Rajput clan who ruled Jhalawar. The district combines cultural heritage of the Malwa region and the Rajputana in western India. With some exquisite pre-historic cave paintings, massive forts, thickly-wooded forests and exotic wildlife variety, Jhalawar boasts of rich historic as well as natural wealth. Culturally, the district is a typical synthesis of Rajasthani and Malwa cultures.

Jhalawar district is an expanse of fertile plain having rich black-cotton soil. It is watered by several rivers, giving it a verdant look. The largest river flowing through the area is Kali Sindh which flows through the territory to join the Chambal, Rajasthan's largest river. Other rivers include Ujaad, Ahu, Parvan, Chavli, etc. The Aravali hills, which are the most ancient folded mountain range in India, cross the region roughly dividing the plains of Hadoti from the Malwa plateau. These hills and the surrounding areas were once thickly forested and teemed with wildlife. The Jhalawar region has an exotic flavor with its diverse range of flora and fauna, with which it is richly-blessed. Red poppy fields add to the vibrant color, while the Saras crane breeding grounds spotlight the rich avian life dominating Jhalawar territory.

The main crops of the district are Jowar, Maize, Wheat, Rice, Gram, Masoor, Dhania, Mustard, Groundnut, Soyabean and Opium. The forest area is about 17.29 per cent of the total land area. The principal trees are Dhak, Dhonkra, Tendu, Kher, Babool and Khejra. The main fruits are Plum, Papaya, Lemon, Mango, Gauva and Orange and in Orange cultivation, the district is known as Chhota Nagpur of Rajasthan.

Jhalawar is industrially a backward district of the state. Even though the district occupies a prime position in the production of soyabean, orange and coriander, agro-processing industry in the district has failed to pick up. The district lacks basic facilities for the development of industries. This includes inadequacy of railway infrastructure, cold storage facilities and a district dairy cooperative.

Most of the water in this highest rainfall district flows out of the district in the absence of water shed development and also leads to soil erosion. Development of watershed, farm bunds and small/ medium irrigation plans are needed to use this water for the district. This is all the more important as five out of six administrative blocks of the district have been declared critical with the state of groundwater development varying between 94 and 110. Only Khanpur block is classified as semi-critical with the stage of groundwater development as 71[11].

District Profile of Jhalawar

Jhalawar has a population of 1,411,327 in 2011 which includes male and female population of 725,667nand 685,660 respectively. In 2001, Jhalawar had a population of 1,180,323 of which males were 612,804 and females were 567, 19. The district population of Jhalawar constituted 2.06 percent of the total population of Rajasthan. As per 2001 census, the proportion to total population of Rajasthan was at 2.09 percent.

The provisional data of Census 2011 depicts that the density of Jhalawar district is 227 people per sq.km. The density in 2001 was at 190 people per sq.km. The district of Jhalawar administers 6,215 sq. kilo meters of areas.

Table 4.9 : Demographic Profile of Jhalawar District

Description	2011	2001
Population	14,11,327	11,80,323
Male	7,25,667	6,12,804
Female	6,85,660	5,67,519
Population Growth	19.57%	30.13%
Area Sq. Km	6,215	6,215
Density/km2	227	190
Proportion to Rajasthan Population	2.06%	2.09%
Average Literacy (%)	62.13	57.32
Male Literacy	76.47	73.31
Female Literacy	47.06	40.02
Rural-Urban Population in 2011	Rural	Urban
Population (%)	83.74%	16.26%
Total Population	11,81,889	2,29,438
Male Population	6,06,823	1,18,844
Female Population	5,75,066	1,10,594

Source: Census of India

The average literacy rate of Jhalawar in 2001 was 57.32 and it increased to 62.13 in 2011. The male and female literacy rate as per census 2011 stood at 76.47 and 47.06 respectively. In 2001 the same was at 73.31 and 40.02. The female literacy rate has made a significant growth in a decade. The total literates in Jhalawar district were 750,039 including 473,018 male and 277,021 females in 2011.

According to Census 2011, 83.74 percent population of Jhalawar lives in rural areas. The total district population living in rural areas is 1,181,889 of which males and females are 606,823 and 575,066 respectively. Out of the total Jhalawar population in 2011 census, 16.26 percent lives in urban regions of district. The census of 2001 revealed that the share of scheduled caste population in Jhalawar is 15.6 percent while the scheduled tribe population is 12.0 percent.

Implementation of MGNREGA in Jhalawar

Jhalawar is also one of the districts where MGNREGA was implemented in the first phase. It has been identified as one of the least developed areas of the country comprising mostly of marginal farmers and forest dwellers. Poverty in this district has increased despite consistent focus of several poverty eradication programmes. [1] With MGNREGA's objectives of job creation with minimum wages and creation of productive assets like water harvesting, road connectivity, land cultivation, etc. Jhalawar was apt to implement MGNREGA in the initial phase.

In Jhalawar, the two blocks, Jhalrapatan and Pirawa were selected through purposive sampling method. Using snowball sampling technique Durgpura *gram panchayat* and Sunel *gram panchayat* were selected from Jhalrapatan and Pirawa respectively.

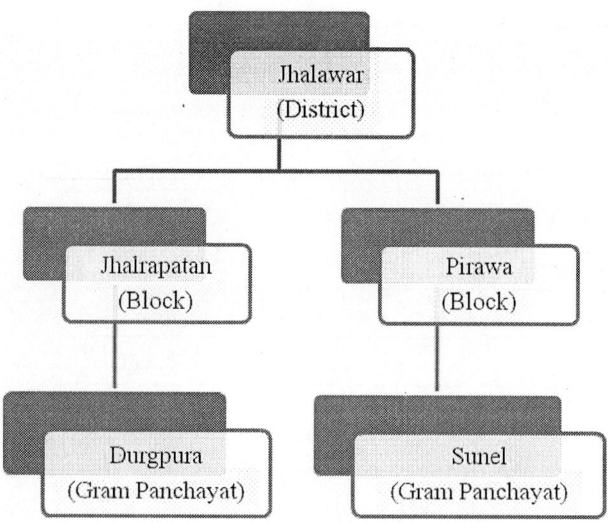

Figure 4.6: Sample of Jhalawar District

In each *gram panchayats* 30 workers were interviewed. The interview in Durgpura was carried out at a worksite near Durgpura village. A road was repaired which was constructed under MGNREGA was in progress. Since there were only few people working at the worksite, interviews of beneficiaries was carried out in the villages of Kotra and Durgpura which comes under Durgpura *gram panchayat*. In Pirawa, there was no work carried out during the field visit. So the interview of the beneficiaries was held in Suhas villageIn total sixty people were interviewed in Jhalawar districts.

Sample Respondents

Out of 30 respondents in Durgpura are 25 are female. The female work participation rate among SC and ST are low as compared to OBC category with 53.3 per cent. Male workforce is very low. In Sunel *gram panchayat,* there was no work carried out as mentioned above. The male or head of the household responded to the questionnaire but it is the women of the household who goes to work under MGNREGA.

Table 4.10: Sample Respondents in Jhalawar

Caste	Male	Female	Total
		Durgpura	
SC	1(3.3)	4(13.3)	5(16.7)
ST	1(3.3)	5(16.7)	6(20)
OBC	3 (10.0)	16(53.3)	19(63.3)
Total	4(13.3)	25(83.3)	30(100)
		Sunel	
SC	12(40)	0	12(40)
ST	11(36.7)	0	11(36.7)
OBC	7(23.3)	0	7(23.3)
Total	30(100)	0	30(100)

Figures in brackets indicates percentage

In both the *gram panchayat,* the workforce is mostly women from the marginalized sections of the society. One of the main objectives of the Act is to aid and empower marginalized sections of the society, which includes, among others, SC, ST, and women. It has been seen that people from the upper castes, particularly those from the general category and Brahmins, do not work under MGNREGA. They consider that working with marginalized sections of the society may affect their social status. In accordance with this, men consider the work of MGNREGA to be meant for women. This is one of the reasons for the large percentage of female workers, with limited days of work and low wage rate under the Act being the other reasons.

Household Size

The size of the household is of significant importance since employment is provided to the household under MGNREGA. The average household size of Durgpura is 3-4. The maximum member in a household is 5-6 which is considered to be small in number as compared to other rural households.

Table 4.11: Household Size of Respondents in Jhalawar

No. of Household members	Frequency	Percent	Cumulative Percent
Durgpura			
1-2	8	26.7	26.7
3-4	17	56.7	83.3
5-6	5	16.7	100
Total	30	100	
Sunel			
1-2	3	10	10
3-4	10	33.3	43.3
5-6	10	33.3	76.7
7-8	1	3.3	80
9-10	3	10	90
10 & above	3	10	100
Total	30	100	

The situation stands different in Sunel, where there are families with more than ten members. A family with large number of members has not benefitted much from the Act. The statute guarantees work to a household for 100 days only which cannot address the needs of family with large number of members. So, these households have to look for other means of livelihood.

Profile of Sample Respondents

The following table 4.12 indicates the background of the respondents' interviewed. In Durgpura out of thirty respondents, twenty four people have a BPL card which is 80 percent of the total sample. Half of the total sample i.e.50 percent of the respondents in

Durgpura are landless labourer. This means that they are dependents on earnings from employment. Those who have a land holding cultivate on their land and seek for MGNREGA employment during the lean season.

Table 4.12 : Profile of Sample Respondent in Jhalawar

Household Income(Monthly)	BPL card holder	Land Holding				Total
		Landless	1-5 Bigha	6-10 Bigha	16-20 Bigha	
Durgpura						
500-1000	Yes	2(6.7)	3(10.0)	0	0	5(16.7)
	No	0	2(6.7)	0	0	2(6.7)
1000-1500	Yes	3(10.0)	0	0	0	3(10.0)
	No	1(3.3)	0	0	0	1(3.3)
1500-2000	Yes	8(26.7)	2(6.7)	0	0	10(33.3)
	No	1(3.3)	0	0	0	1(3.3)
2000-2500	Yes	1(3.3)	1(3.3)	0	1(3.3)	3(10.0)
2500-3000	Yes	1(3.3)	1(3.3)	1(3.3)	0	3(10.0)
	No	0	0	0	1(3.3)	1(3.3)
4000 & above	No	0	0	0	1(3.3)	1(3.3)
Total		17(56.6)	9(30.0)	1(3.3)	3(10.0)	30(100)
Sunel						
Household Income(Monthly)	**BPL card holder**	Land Holding				**Total**
		Landless	**1-5 Bigha**	**6-10 Bigha**	**11-15 Bigha**	
500-1000	Yes	5(16.7)	1(3.3)	1(3.3)	0	7(23.3)
	No	1(3.3)	15(50.0)	0	0	16(53.3)
1000-1500	Yes	1(3.3)	2(6.7)	0	0	3(10.0)
	No	1(3.3)	0	0	1(3.3)	2(6.7)
1500-2000	Yes	1(3.3)	0	0	0	1(3.3)
	No	0	0	0	1(3.3)	1(3.3)
Total		9(30.0)	18(60.0)	1(3.3)	2(6.7)	30(100)

Figures in brackets indicates percentage

Unlike Durgpura, the number of people with BPL card is less in Sunel. Only 13.3 per cent have a BPL card despite the fact that they fall under the BPL category. The optimistic aspect is that out of the 30 workers, 21 people have land from which they get a decent income for their survival. The household monthly income of most of the workers ranges between Rs. 500–1000.

Awareness Level

In both the *panchayats,* people were aware about MGNREGA but not of the provisions of the Act. *Gram sabhas* are the main decision making and implementing agency in MGNREGA. All the announcements and planning of the Act is done by the *gram sabha.* It is also the responsibility of the *gram sabha* to conduct social audit of the work taken up by the *gram panchayat.*

However, as can be seen from Table 4.13 below, only 30 per cent of the respondents in Durgpura and 13.3 per cent in Sunel were aware about *gram sabha* held in the villages. A majority of the population (26.6 per cent) in Durgpura said that *gram sabha* is held among the panchayat members only, and villagers are not involved in the process. In Sunel, 63.3 per cent said that no *gram sabha* was held since the time MGNREGA came into force, and 16.6 per cent had no idea what a *gram sabha* was.

Table 4.13: Awareness Among the Respondents About the Provisions of the Act in Jhalawar

Educational Qualification	Gram Sabha held				Source of Information about the Act		Signed Receipt after applying for Job		Unemployment Allowance	
	Yes	Yes (only Panchayat members)	No	No Idea	Villagers	Panchayat members	Yes	No	Yes	No
Durgpura										
Illiterate	7 (23.3)	7 (23.3)	4 (6.6)	9 (30.0)	9 (30.0)	18 (60.0)	2 (6.6)	25 (83.3)	0	27 (90.0)
Class I-V	0	1 (3.3)	0	0	0	1 (3.3)	0	1 (3.3)	0	1 (3.3)
Class VI-VIII	1 (3.3)	0	0	0	1 (3.3)	0	0	1 (3.3)	0	1 (3.3)
Senior Secondary	1 (3.3)	0	0	0	0	1 (3.3)	0	1 (3.3)	0	1 (3.3)
Total	9 (30.0)	8 (26.6)	4 (6.6)	9 (30.0)	10 (33.3)	2 (6.6)	2 (6.6)	28 (93.3)	0	30 (100)
Sunel										
Illiterate	1 (3.3)	0	9 (30.0)	2 (6.6)	0	12 (40.0)	0	7 (23.3)	0	7 (23.3)
	2 (6.6)	1 (3.3)	6 (20.0)	2 (6.6)	0	11 (36.7)	1 (3.3)	11 (36.7)	0	12 (40.0)
	1 (3.3)	1 (3.3)	4 (6.6)	1 (3.3)	0	7 (23.3)	0	11 (36.7)	0	11 (36.7)
Total	4 (6.6)	2 (6.6)	19 (63.3)	5 (16.6)	0	30 (100)	1 (3.3)	29 (96.6)	0	30 (100)

Figures in brackets indicates percentage

In both the *gram panchayats*, the majority of the population got the information about the Act from the panchayat members. It was found that no hoardings, padyatras, street plays, etc., were held to spread the awareness regarding the Act. In both Durgpura and Sunel, only posters were displayed in the office of the *gram panchayat* to spread awareness.

In Durgpura, only 2 out of 30 persons had received a signed receipt after applying for the job. Similarly, in Sunel only one person got a signed receipt after applying for the job. It was surprising to find that none of the respondents were aware about the

Unemployment Allowances, which should be provided if work is not provided within 15 days of demand for work. There is always a delay in providing employment after applying for work. Lack of awareness about the Act is one of the major lacunae in the proper implementation of the Act.

Duration of Getting a Job Card and Job after Applying

The duration of getting a Job Card (JC) after applying and getting a job after applying is usually more than a month in both the *gram panchayats*. The respondents have also complained that they do not get a job for months after applying for it. They don't get an unemployment allowance because they are unaware of the provision.

Table 4.14: Duration of Getting Job Card and Job after Applying in Jhalawar

Days	Durgpura		Sunel	
	Duration of getting JC	On Demand-Job Duration	Duration of getting JC	On Demand-Job Duration
10-15 days	5 (16.6)	5 (16.6)	1 (3.3)	4 (13.3)
15-20 days	1(3.3)	0	3 (10.0)	1 (3.3)
25-30 days	2 (6.6)	12 (40.0)	8 (26.6)	16 (53.3)
30 & above	22 (73.3)	13(43.3)	18(60.0)	9(30.0)
Total	30(100)	30(100)	30(100)	30(100)

Figures in brackets indicates percentage

In Durgpura, 73.3 per cent of the total workers got a JC after a month from the date of registration. Only 16.6 per cent got a job within 15 days of application and the remaining got a job only after 15 days. The situation in Sunel is also similar to Durgpura. They don't get employment on demand while the approach of the policy is on-demand job.

It was observed that there is a social system in getting a job. The sarpanch (or panchayat members) decides who will be given a job. Jobs are provided on priority basis to those people who have cordial relations with the panchayat members. This is one of the main reasons that people do not complain. In case they complain, their future prospect of getting a job becomes leaner. On questioning about the issue, the panchayat secretary said that there is not enough work to gratify the demands of the beneficiary so they give jobs to those households who are economically poor.

Number of Days Worked by the Respondents in the Financial Year 2010-11

Under MGNREGA a household should be provided 100 days of guaranteed employment in a financial year. Work should be provided as and when demanded by any member of the household registered in the Job Card.

It has been found that there is lack of work in both the *gram panchayat* to address the demand for employment by the people. The graph below indicates number of days the workers have worked under the Act in the financial year 2010–11.

Figure 4.7: No of Days worked by the respondents in financial year 2010–11 in Jhalawar

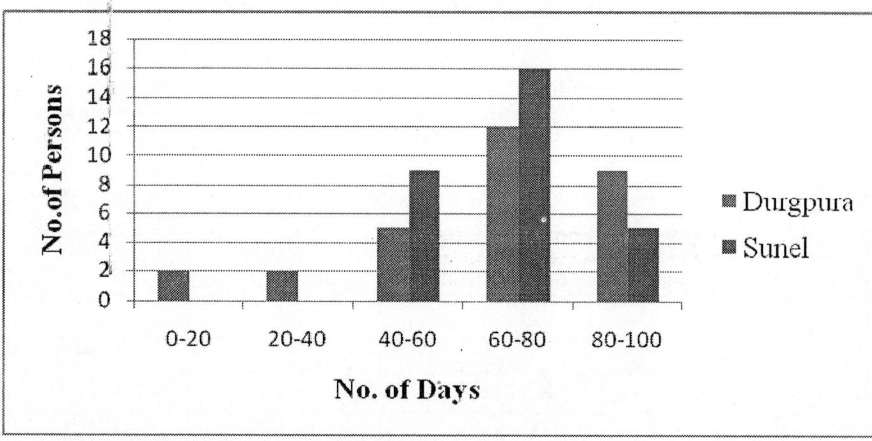

In both the *gram panchayat*, the average days worked by the beneficiaries is 60–80 days. None of the respondents in Durgpura completed 100 days of guaranteed employment whereas in Sunel only 5 (16.6 per cent) have completed 100 days. Since the enactment of MGNREGA, many sections of the society have been demanding an increase in the 100 days of employment. Yet, the guaranteed 100 days of work is also not provided to workers on demand. The sustainability of the Act to provide guaranteed work on demand is the big question.

The basic entitlement of the Act is to provide 100 days of work. The findings from the field show that workers are willing to work for more than 100 days. The issue is lack of work to meet the demand of the job seeker. The PRI are unable to generate work for the people. The capacity of the PRI functionaries needs to strengthened. It was also found that PRI functionaries are not trained properly which is one of the reasons that they are unable to create enough work to address the demand for work.

Payment Related Issues

There are issues of delay in payment in both the *gram panchayat.* Many villagers have complained during the field visit that their payments are not made on time. Delay in payment and payment of less wage has been one of the areas of concern in the implementation of MGNREGA.

Table 4.15: Payment Related Issues in Jhalawar

Gram Panchayat	Durgpura	Sunel
Payment Received per day (in Rs.)		
60–70	3 (10)	2 (6.6)
70–80	4 (13.3)	24 (80)
80–90	2 (6.6)	2 (6.6)
90–100	3 (10)	0
100 & above	18 (60)	2 (6.6)
Total	30(100)	30(100)
Frequency of Payment(in months)		
15 days–1 month	5 (16.6)	5 (16.6)
1–2 months	19 (63.3)	23 (76.6)
2–3 months	4 (13.3)	2 (6.6)
3–6 months	2 (6.6)	0
Total	30(100)	30(100)

Figures in brackets indicate percentage

The above table shows that in Durgpura the maximum number of respondents has received a payment of Rs. 100–110 whereas in Sunel only 2 (6.6 per cent) people received a payment of Rs. 100–110. There was no discrimination in the payment made to women. The issue is that payments are made through bank accounts which are in the name of the male head of the household. Therefore, women who do the actual work are at times deprived of the financial benefits of their own hard labour.

In Sunel, most of the beneficiaries are getting only Rs. 70–80, which is less than what they have been assured. In both the *gram panchayat*, there was a major problem of delay in payment. From January 2011 till March 2011, beneficiaries didn't receive their payment in Durgpura, whereas the officials claimed that payment was being made on time. Similarly, in Sunel people go to their bank which is 20–25 km from their villages, only to find that the money has not come. In Sunel, the panchayat secretary puts the blame on the district and higher authorities who do not release funds on time. And thus the blame game goes on and on.

In both the *gram panchayat*, people refrain from filing any complaint against non-availability of work and delay in payment. They fear that if they file any complaint, their future prospect of getting work will be doomed. Some beneficiaries have also complained that they are not paid full payment, though according to the *panchayat* secretary payments are made according to the work done.

Worksite Related Issues

Under the Act, work is to be provided within 5 km of the village. If work is not provided within 5 km, extra wages of 10 per cent are payable to meet additional transportation and living expenses. Nonetheless the table below reveals a different story.

Table 4.16: Worksite Related Issues in Jhalawar

Gram Panchayats	Durgpura	Sunel
Distance of worksite(in km)		
1 km	1(3.3)	0
2 km	5(16.7)	9(30.0)
3 km	6(20.0)	11(36.7)
4 km	4(13.3)	0
5 km	9(30.0)	6(20.0)
6 km	5(16.7)	4(13.3)
Total	30(100)	30(100)
Worksite Facilities		
Nothing	10(33.3)	1(3.3)
Shade	12(40.0)	4(13.3)
Water	0	8(26.7)
Water and Medical Aid	0	4(13.3)
Water and Shade	8(26.7)	13(43.3)
Total	30(100)	30(100)

Figures in brackets indicate percentage

In Durgpura, 16.7 per cent of the population goes to work beyond

5 km, which entitles them to an additional 10 per cent of the wage rate as transport and living allowance. But in both the *panchayats,* no one was paid such an allowance. A large percentage (30.0) of the respondents comes from a distance of 5 km. Similarly, in Sunel 13.3 per cent come from a distance of 6 km where the workers are unaware about the entitlement for transport. Majority of the respondents, that is, 40 per cent, in Durgpura said that only shade has been provided at the worksite. Out of the total workers, 33.3 per cent said that no worksite facilities are provided in Durgpura while 26.6 per cent responded that shade and water is provided at the worksite. In Sunel, 43.3 per cent responded that shade and water have been provided. Unlike Durgpura, 13.3 per cent workers told that water and medical aid is provided at the worksites in Sunel. However it was observed during the visit to the worksite that crèche facility was missing. Despite majority of the workers being women with young children, crèche facility has not been provided.

Overall Observation

The implementation level at both the *gram panchayats* was more or less the same. In both the *gram panchayats,* people were unaware of their rights under the Act. They were only aware that work will be provided to those who have a Job Card. Many of them were unable to tell how many days they have worked under the scheme. They were also unable to calculate their wages. It is the mate who decides about their payment and they happily accept whatever the mate give them. There are no awareness campaigns done to raise awareness among the workers. Many of the respondents and villagers complained that there is lack of work. Work is not provided when they demand for it. The PRI functionaries remain ignorant about the fact. Implementing agencies were not much aware about the implementation of the Act. The *panchayat* secretary of Jhalrapatan hardly visits the villages under his *panchayat.* His assistant looks after all his work and responded to most of the questions during the interview. The *panchayat* secretary was unaware about the ground realities.

Sirohi

Sirohi district is situated at the south-west part of Rajasthan between parallel of 24° 20' and 25° 17' North Latitude and 72° 16' and 73° 10' East Longitude. It is bordered on the west by Jalor District, on the north by Pali District, on the east by Udaipur District, and on the south by Banas Kantha District of Gujarat. The district has an area of 5136 sq.km.

It is the administrative headquarters of Sirohi district, and was formerly the capital of the princely state of the same name ruled by Deora Rajput. It has five tehsils (administrative division): Abu Road, Sheoganj, Reodar, Pindwara and Sirohi.

Sirohi district is broken up by hills and rocky ranges. The granite mass of Mount Abu divides the district into two portions, running from north-east to south-west. The south and south-east part of the district, which lies between Mount Abu and the main spine of the Aravallis, is mountainous and rugged, and is drained by the West Banas River. Abu Road, a station on the main Delhi-Ahmedabad rail line, lies in the valley of the West Banas. Dry deciduous forest is common in this part of the district, and the higher elevations of Mount Abu are covered in conifer forests. Abu Road is the biggest city and the main financial hub of Sirohi district. Sirohi district has least number of villages in Rajasthan.

The portion of the district west and north of Mount Abu is drier, lying in the rain shadow of the mountain, which blocks the southwest monsoon. The southwest corner of the district is drained by the Sukri River, an intermittent stream that drains the western slope of Mount Abu. The north western portion of the district is drained by tributaries of the Luni River. The north western thorn scrub forests cover the western and northern portion of the district. Warada is the last village of Sirohi located on Sirohi-Siyana Road.

The name Sirohi had been derived by "Siranwa" hills on the Western slope on which it stands. Colonel Tod in his book "Travels in Western India" has suggested that the names of the territory might have derived from its position at the head (Sir) of the desert (Rohi). Sirohi also named as "Sword" and this had led some people to believe that this State of brave Deora Chauhans received its present name due to the wide spread fame of its Swords[2]. Sirohi is also called as "Dev Nagari" since ancient times because of many temples and shrines in the district.

In 1405, Rao Sobha Ji (sixth in descent from Rao Deoraj, the Progenitor of the Deora Clan of Chauhans) founded a town Shivpuri on eastern slope of Siranwa hill which is called Khuba. A relic of the old city is found there and a pious place of Virji is still a place of worship.

Sehastramal, the son of Rao Sobha ji founded the present city Sirohi on western slope and laid the foundation stone of the Sirohi fort on the second day of Vaisakh in the year 1482 i.e. 1425 (A.D.)

on the top the present town of Sirohi and made it his capital. It lies on the western slope of the Siranwa hills, later all the area under Deoras came to be known as Sirohi. In puranic tradition this area has always been referred to as "Arbudh Pradesh". It was also sometimes known as Arbudanchal.

Figure 4.8: Map of Sirohi

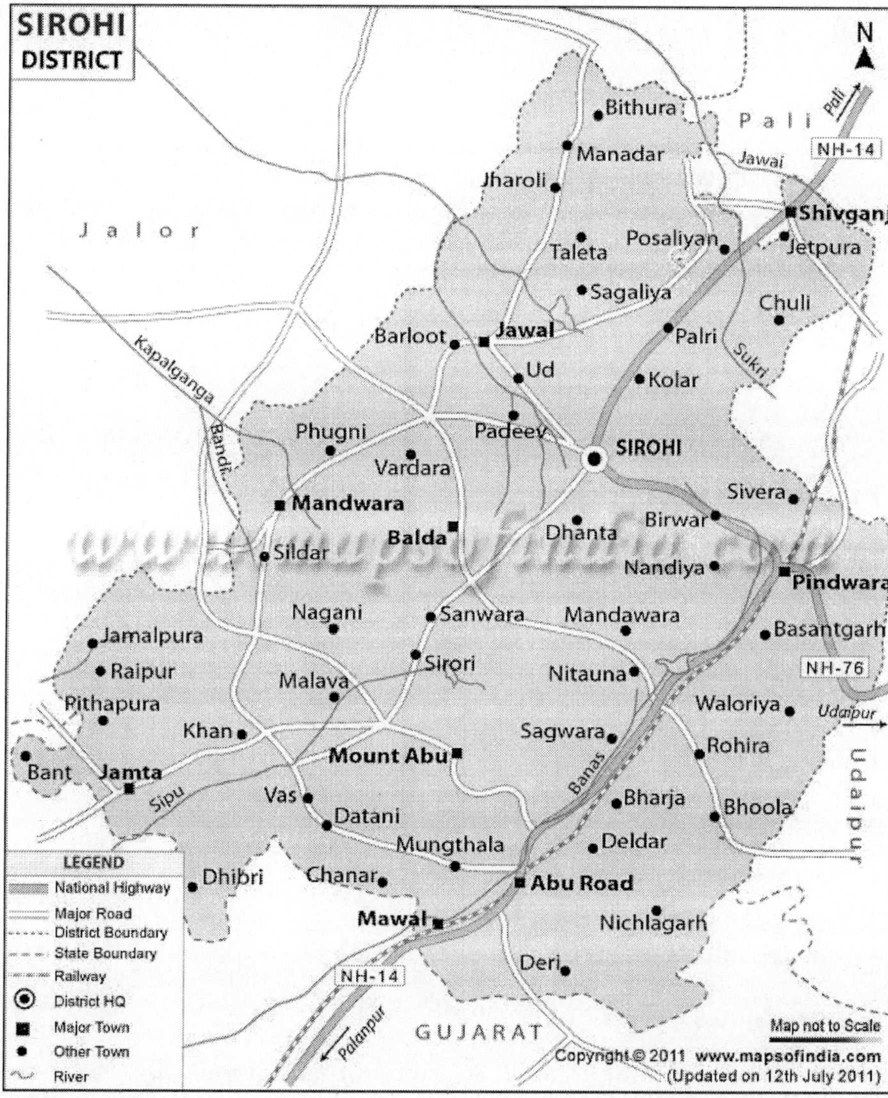

Source: www.mapsofindia.com

After Independence, an agreement was signed between the Central government and the minor ruler of Sirohi State. With this, the State administration of the Sirohi state was taken over by Bombay Government from 5th January 1949 to 25th January 1950. After the final merger with Rajasthan in 1950, an area of 787 sq. km. consisting of Abu road and Delwara tehsils of Sirohi district was renamed with the Bombay State on 01, Nov. 1956, after the recommendation of the State organisation Commission, which forms the present position of the district.

District Profile of Sirohi

The census data of 2011 reveals that the population of Sirohi is 1,037,185 which include male and female population of 535,115 and 502,070 respectively. In comparison the 2001 data shows that Sirohi had a population of 851,107 of which males were 437,949 and remaining 413,158 were females.

Table 4.17 : Demographic Profile of Sirohi District

Description	2011	2001
Population	10,37,185	8,51,107
Male	5,35,115	4,37,949
Female	5,02,070	4,13,158
Population Growth	21.86%	26.81%
Area Sq. Km	5,131	5,131
Density/km^2	202	166
Proportion to Rajasthan Population	1.51%	1.51%
Average Literacy (%)	56.02	53.94
Male Literacy	71.09	69.89
Female Literacy	40.12	37.15
Rural-Urban Population in 2011	Rural	Urban
Population (%)	79.87%	20.13%
Total Population	8,28,375	2,08,810
Male Population	4,24,973	1,10,142
Female Population	4,03,402	98,668

Source: Census of India

There was change of 21.86 percent in the population compared to the population as per 2001 census. In the previous census of India 2001, Sirohi district recorded an increase of 26.81 percent to its population compared to 1991.

According to the provisional data of census 2011, the density of Sirohi district is 202 people per sq.km. The same in 2001 was 166 people per sq.km. The total population of Sirohi constituted 1.51 percent of Rajasthan population both in 2001 and 2011.

In 2011 Census the average literacy rate of Sirohi was 56.02. The average literacy rate in 2001 was 53.94. The male literacy rate in 2001 was 69.89 and it increased to 71.09 in 2011. Similarly, the female literacy rate in 2001 was 37.15 which increased in 2011 to 40.12.

In census 2011 the rural population in Sirohi district have been recorded at 79.87 percent. The total population of people living in rural areas of Sirohi is 828,375 of which males and females are 424,973 and 403,402 respectively. As per Census 2011, the total percentage of people who live in urban regions of the district is 20.13. Out of the total urban population of 208,810, males are 110,142 and females are 98,668. The SC population in Sirohi is 19.15 percent and ST population is 24.76 percent in 2001 census.

Implementation of MGNREGA in Sirohi

As has been discussed earlier, MGNREGA was implemented in a phased manner. Sirohi is one of the backward districts out of the six districts, where the scheme was introduced in the first phase. It is one of the poorest districts in Rajasthan with about 31 percent of the population living below the poverty line. It is also one of the districts close to Gujarat, where large scale migration takes place during drought. This is one of the reasons for implementing MGNREGA in Sirohi during the first phase in Rajasthan.

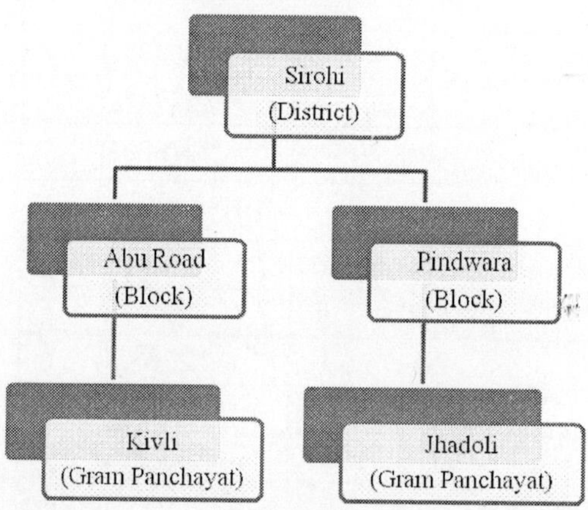

Figure 4.9: Sample of Sirohi District

The two blocks of Sirohi i.e. Abu Road and Pindwara were selected through purposive sampling method. Using snowball sampling technique, Kivli *gram panchayat* was selected in Abu Road and Jhadoli *gram panchayat* was opted in Pindwara block.

The interview of 30 workers in Kivli was conducted at two worksites. In the first worksite, a building to be used as *gram panchayat's* office was in progress. Semi-skilled workers were also working under MGNREGA in that worksite. At the other worksite, a road which was constructed earlier under MGNREGA was being repaired.

In Jhadoli, 30 beneficiaries were interviewed at a worksite where more than 40 people were working. In the worksite, digging work was in progress to harvest water. In this area, there is scarcity of water. The villagers go through a lot of problems because of inadequate water. A total of sixty beneficiaries were interviewed in Sirohi district.

Sample Respondents

The following table shows the distribution of workers according to gender and caste. The samples comprises mostly of women in both the *gram panchayats.* One of the major objectives of the Act is to bring equality whether gender-wise or class wise. MGNREGA is an opportunity to decrease the disparity existing in the society.

Table 4.18: Sample Respondents in Sirohi

Caste	Male	Female	Total
		Kivli	
SC	4(13.3)	10(33.3)	14(46.7)
ST	0	3(10.0)	3(10.0)
OBC	1(3.3)	10(33.3)	11(36.7)
General	1(3.3)	1(3.3)	2(6.7)
Total	6(20.0)	24(80.0)	30(100)
		Jhadoli	
SC	1(3.3)	3(10.0)	4(13.3)
ST	1(3.3)	7(23.3)	8(26.7)
OBC	2(6.7)	12(40.0)	14(46.7)
General	3(10.0)	1(3.3)	4(13.3)
Total	7(23.3)	23(76.6)	30(100)

Figures in brackets indicates percentage

In Kivli, the male work participation is very low as compared to female. Like other two districts discussed above, the number of female workers are more. The maximum number of workforce is from SC category. People from general caste category are very low with only 6.7 percent of the total sample.

Like Kivli, the workforce in Jhadoli also comprises mostly of female workers. The highest work participation is from OBC category with 46.7 percent. The lowest work participation was from SC and general caste. In Sirohi, unlike Dungarpur and Jhalawar where people from general category are reluctant to work under MGNREGA, people from general category also work under MGNREGA. This indicates that all sections of the society have access to work under the Act.

Household Size

In Sirohi the benefit from MGNREGA employment is significant. With fewer members in a family, the income from MGNREGA is significant. Nobody complained about work being given for 100 days to a household and not to individuals as in the case of other districts.

Table 4.19: Household Size of Respondents in Sirohi

No. of Household members	Frequency	Percent	Cumulative Percent
Kivli			
1-2	9	30.0	30.0
3-4	8	26.7	56.7
5-6	9	30.0	86.7
7-8	4	13.3	100.0
Total	30	100	
Jhadoli			
1-2	7	23.3	23.3
3-4	7	23.3	46.7
5-6	12	40.0	86.7
7-8	4	13.3	100.0
Total	30	100.0	

The maximum number of members in a household in Kivli is 7-8. But only a small percentage i.e.13.3 percent has a family household of 7-8 members. Most of the beneficiaries have family members ranging between 1-2 or 5-6.

In Jhadoli, the average size of a family is 5-6. Similarly with Kivli, only 13.3 percent have 7-8 members in a family. Generally, the size of a household is small in this area. The children of the house abandon their parents. It has been seen that many elderly people are working under MGNREGA because their children have left them to look after themselves.

Profile of the Sample Respondents

MGNREGA is meant to provide livelihood security to the poor. The policy is a pro-poor policy and benefits of it should be reached to the poor in rural areas. Among the people who have been interviewed there are people whose household members are government employee working as teachers, post masters and retired government employees. Since there is limited work created in the area, the poor stand a bleak chance of getting employment opportunities. The main flaw in the Act is that there should be certain criteria to identify the poor household and work should be given on priority basis.

The table below gives a glimpse on the profile of the workers who have been interviewed in Sirohi. This will enable us to assess the impact of the policy on the lives of the people.

Table 4.20: Profile of Sample Respondents in Sirohi

Household Income(Monthly)	BPL card holder	Land Holding			Total
		Landless	1-5 Bigha	11-15 Bigha	
Kivli					
Only MGNREGA wage	Yes	5(16.7)	0	0	5(16.7)
	No	0	2(6.7)	0	2(6.7)
500-1000	Yes	1(3.3)	0	0	1(3.3)
1000-1500	No	3(10.0)	1(3.3)	0	4(13.3)
1500-2000	Yes	1(3.3)	0	0	1(3.3)
	No	1(3.3)	0	1(3.3)	1(3.3)
2000-2500	Yes	1(3.3)	0	0	1(3.3)
	No	0	1(3.3)	0	1(3.3)
2500-3000	Yes	0	1(3.3)	0	1(3.3)
	No	1(3.3)	0	0	1(3.3)
3000-3500	Yes	1(3.3)	0	0	1(3.3)
	No	2(6.7)	1(3.3)	0	3(10.0)
4000 & above	Yes	3(10.0)	2(6.7)	0	5(16.7)
	No	1(3.3)	1(3.3)	0	2(6.7)
Total		20(66.7)	9(30.0)	1(3.3)	30(100)

Household Income(Monthly)	BPL card holder	Land Holding		Total
Jhadoli				
		Landless	1-5 Bigha	
Only MGNREGA wage	Yes	1(3.3)	0	1(3.3)
	No	6(20.0)	2(6.7)	8(26.7)
500-1000	Yes	1(3.3)	0	1(3.3)
	No	1(3.3)	0	1(3.3)
1000-1500	No	0	2(6.7)	2(6.7)
1500-2000	No	2(6.7)	3(10.0)	5(16.7)
2000-2500	No	2(6.7)	4(13.3)	6(20.0)
2500-3000	No	1(3.3)	0	1(3.3)
3000-3500	Yes	1(3.3)	1(3.3)	2(6.7)
	No	1(3.3)	0	1(3.3)
4000 & above	No	2(6.7)	0	2(6.7)
Total		18(60.0)	12(40.0)	30(100)

Figures in brackets indicates percentage

In Kivli, half of the total sample population are BPL card holders. The remaining population also comes under the BPL category but they are not registered under the BPL category. Out of the total population, 66.7 percent in Kivli are landless workers. For them the work provided under MGNREGA is a fortunate thing. Here, 23.3 percent of the workers are dependent totally on MGNREGA wage. The positive impact on the lives of those who are entirely dependent on MGNREGA is clearly visible. Many of them responded that with MGNREGA at least they get a square meal without going out of the village to work.

The economic status in Jhadoli is shoddier than workers in Kivli. In Jhadoli, 60 percent of the sampled workers are landless labourer while the remaining 40 percent have only 1-5 Bigha land. Around 30 percent of the workers were dependent on MGNREGA wages for their livelihood. Despite their low economic status, only 5 out of 30 have a BPL card.

Awareness Level

The beneficiaries were well aware about MGNREGA. This awareness can be attributed to the proactive role of Rajasthan in the enactment of the right to work. Yet, the awareness level among the beneficiaries about the provisions of the Act is low. This confines their capacity to benefit completely from the Act. The beneficiaries are not aware regarding the meetings and low participation at *gram sabhas* which will further deteriorate the situation. The table below gives an idea about the awareness level among the workers regarding the provisions of the Act.

The awareness among the respondents in Kivli and Jhadoli is not different from the other two districts discussed above. Workers were only aware of the work being provided under the Act. In both the *gram panchayats,* awareness regarding the detailed entitlement and benefits of the Act was very low. The low literacy level among the beneficiaries can be one of the reasons for it. In Kivli, 73.3 percent of the workers are illiterate and the percentage for the same in Jhadoli is 90 percent.

Gram sabha is a platform to discuss the developmental issues of the village and also to disseminate information regarding various policies. Planning and choice of work to be taken up in the village are all to be discussed and decided at *gram sabha.* The workers can get all the information regarding the Act from the meetings.

Table 4.21: Awareness Among the Respondents About the Provisions of the Act in Sirohi

Household Income(Monthly)	BPL card holder	Land Holding			Total
		Landless	1-5 Bigha	11-15 Bigha	
Kivli					
Only MGNREGA wage	Yes	5(16.7)	0	0	5(16.7)
	No	0	2(6.7)	0	2(6.7)
500-1000	Yes	1(3.3)	0	0	1(3.3)
1000-1500	No	3(10.0)	1(3.3)	0	4(13.3)
1500-2000	Yes	1(3.3)	0	0	1(3.3)
	No	1(3.3)	0	1(3.3)	1(3.3)
2000-2500	Yes	1(3.3)	0	0	1(3.3)
	No	0	1(3.3)	0	1(3.3)
2500-3000	Yes	0	1(3.3)	0	1(3.3)
	No	1(3.3)	0	0	1(3.3)
3000-3500	Yes	1(3.3)	0	0	1(3.3)
	No	2(6.7)	1(3.3)	0	3(10.0)
4000 & above	Yes	3(10.0)	2(6.7)	0	5(16.7)
	No	1(3.3)	1(3.3)	0	2(6.7)
Total		20(66.7)	9(30.0)	1(3.3)	30(100)

Jhadoli

Household Income(Monthly)	BPL card holder	Land Holding		Total
		Landless	1-5 Bigha	
Only MGNREGA wage	Yes	1(3.3)	0	1(3.3)
	No	6(20.0)	2(6.7)	8(26.7)
500-1000	Yes	1(3.3)	0	1(3.3)
	No	1(3.3)	0	1(3.3)
1000-1500	No	0	2(6.7)	2(6.7)
1500-2000	No	2(6.7)	3(10.0)	5(16.7)
2000-2500	No	2(6.7)	4(13.3)	6(20.0)
2500-3000	No	1(3.3)	0	1(3.3)
3000-3500	Yes	1(3.3)	1(3.3)	2(6.7)
	No	1(3.3)	0	1(3.3)
4000 & above	No	2(6.7)	0	2(6.7)
Total		18(60.0)	12(40.0)	30(100)

Figures in brackets indicates percentage

Half of the total workers in Kivli said that *gram sabhas* were held. However, 30 percent in Kivli said that *gram sabha* was held only among *panchayat* members and 20 percent did not have any clue whether *gram sabhas* were held or not. The sources of information on the Act are the members of *panchayats.* Only few of them got the information on the Act from other villagers who have benefitted. A signed receipt with date should be given after applying for job by the authority. A large percentage (83.3%) of the beneficiaries did not get any signed receipt after applying for job. While two qualified people were among those who received a signed receipt. Neither in Kivli nor in Jhadoli people were aware about unemployment allowance which is to be provided if work is not provided within the stipulated time.

In Jhadoli, 39.9 percent said that *gram sabha* was held while 33.3 per cent said that it was not held. Some of them were not aware whether *gram sabhas* were held or not. A majority of the total sample got the information about the Act from the *panchayat* members. 86.6 percent of the total sample did not get a signed receipt after applying for job. They were not aware that the signed receipt with date entitles them to unemployment allowances if work is not provided within the stipulated time.

Duration of Getting a Job Card and Job after Applying

The duration of getting a job card after registration and on demand job is fifteen days.In case a worker do not get work within 15 days, he is entitled for unemployment allowance. Since the workers are not aware of the provision, they do not demand for it.

Table 4.22 : Duration of Getting Job Card and Job after Applying in Sirohi

Education Qualification	Gram Sabha held				Source of Information about the Act		Signed Receipt after applying for Job		Unemployment Allowance	
	Yes	Yes (only Panchayat members)	No	No Idea	Villagers	Panchayat members	Yes	No	Yes	No
Kivli										
Illiterate	10 (33.3)	7 (23.3)	0	5 (16.7)	5 (16.7)	17 (56.6)	3 (10.0)	19 (63.3)	0	22 (73.3)
I-V Class	0	1 (3.3)	0	0	0	1 (3.3)	0	1 (3.3)	0	1 (3.3)
VI-VIII Class	5 (16.7)	0	0	0	0	5 (16.7)	0	5 (16.7)	0	5 (16.7)
Secondary	0	0	0	1 (3.3)	0	1 (3.3)	1 (3.3)	0	0	1 (3.3)
Sr. Secondary	0	1 (3.3)	0	0	0	1 (3.3)	1 (3.3)	0	0	1 (3.3)
Total	15 (50.0)	9 (30.0)	0	6 (20.0)	5 (16.7)	25 (83.3)	5 (16.7)	25 (83.3)	0	30 (100)
Jhadoli										
Illiterate	11 (36.6)	0	9 (30.0)	7 (23.3)	5 (16.7)	22 (73.3)	4 (13.3)	23 (76.6)	0	27 (90.0)
I-V Class	0	0	0	1 (3.3)	0	1 (3.3)	0	1 (3.3)	0	1 (3.3)
VI-VIII Class	0	0	1 (3.3)	0	0	1 (3.3)	0	1 (3.3)	0	1 (3.3)
Secondary	1 (3.3)	0	0	0	1(3.3)	0	0	1 (3.3)	0	1 (3.3)
Total	12 (39.9)	0	10 (33.3)	8 (26.6)	6 (20.0)	24 (80.0)	4 (13.3)	26 (86.6)	0	30 (100)

Figures in brackets indicates percentage

The average days of getting a job card after registering is more than 30 days in Kivli. Similar is the case in Jhadoli where 90 percent got a job card after 30 days. Work is not provided on demand in both the *gram panchayats.* The above table reflects that there is delay in providing employment to the people.

Number of Days Worked by the respondents in the Financial Year 2010-11

MGNREGA is meant to provide 100 days of guaranteed employment to rural households for 100 days in a financial year. It means that work should be provided on demand by the household. There should be enough work created to cater the demand of the rural poor. The table below reveals the number of days a person has worked in the financial year 2010-11

Figure 4.10: No of Days Worked By the Respondents in Financial Year 2010-11 in Sirohi

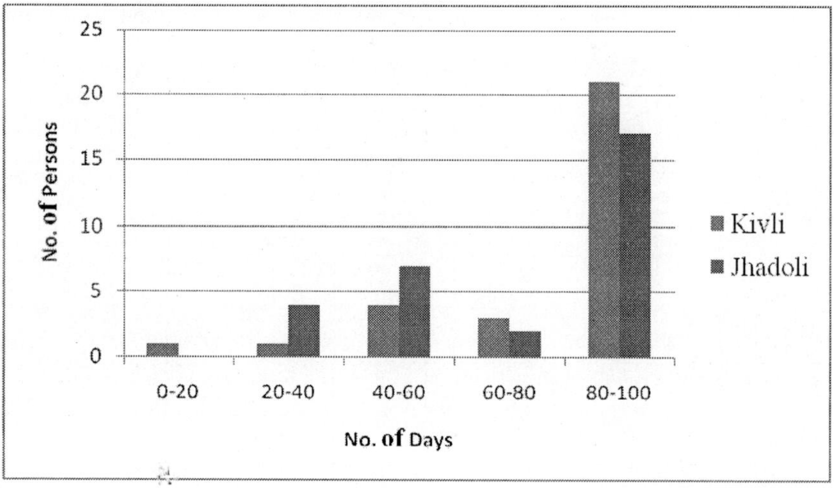

In the financial year 2010-11, maximum number of people in both the Kivli and Jhadoli *gram panchayats* worked for was 80-100 days. It is noteworthy that the people have access to work in this area. They are getting job for 100 days in a financial year. Many of the beneficiaries have completed 100 days of employment provided by the policy. It has been found that most of the workers who have completed 100 days of employment are those who are totally dependent on MGNREGA income for their livelihood. Despite flaws in the implementation of the Act, it has been able to bring positive effect in the lives of the poor and vulnerable. Many of the respondents have suggested that the limit of 100 days should be increased.

Payment Related Issues

The aim of the Act is to provide income or additional income to the rural households. The wage provided should be sufficient to meet the basic requirements of a household and provide livelihood security. However, there are incidences of discrepancy in payments as well as delay in payment. Payments are not timely. The *panchayat* functionaries blame the government officials for the delay in payments. According to the B.D.O., payments are disbursed as soon as the financial sanctions are approved by the competent authorities.

Table 4.23 : Payment Related Issues in Sirohi

Gram Panchayat	Kivli	Jhadoli
Payment Received per day (in Rs.)		
60-70	0	0
70-80	0	1(3.3)
80-90	2(6.7)	1(3.3)
90-100	6(20.0)	10(33.3)
100-110	22(73.3)	18(60.0)
Total	30(100)	30(100)
Frequency of Payment(in months)		
15 days-1 month	18(60.0)	7(23.3)
1-2 months	12(40.0)	22(73.3)
2-3 months	0	1(3.3)
Total	30(100)	30(100)

Figures in brackets indicates percentage

The lowest wage received per day in Kivli is Rs. 80 per day and the higher range is Rs. 110. Wages are paid equally to both men and women. There is no discrimination on the payment of wage. The payment of wages is made according to the measurement of the work done. Around 73 percent of the population in Kivli got payment between Rs.100-110 per day. 60 percent of the total sample in Kivli got their payment between 15 days and one month while the remaining 40 percent got the payment after a month and less than two months time.

In Jhadoli, the minimum wage was Rs. 70 per day and the maximum was similar to Kivli. A large proportion of the sample (60%) received payment of Rs. 100-110 in a day. Many of elderly workers complained that they are paid less wage as compared to other workers. According to the *panchayat* members, many of the workers are elderly women who cannot complete their work in a day, so they are paid minimum wage only. The frequency of payment in Jhadoli is worst than Kivli. Most of the workers receive their payment after a month and less than two months.

Worksite related Issue

There are certain provisions to be provided at the worksite. Worksite facilities such as crèche, drinking water, first aid medical box, etc. have to be provided. The table below depicts the ground reality of the two *gram panchayats*

Table 4.24 : Worksite Related Issues in Sirohi

Gram Panchayats	Kivli	Jhadoli
Distance of worksite(in kms)		
1 km	9(30.0)	5(16.7)
2 km	6(20.0)	9(30.0)
3 km	5(16.7)	6(20.0)
4 km	3(10.0)	7(23.3)
5 km	5(16.7)	3(10.0)
6 km	1(3.3)	0
7 km	1(3.3)	0
Total	30(100)	30(100)
Worksite Facilities		
Nothing	27(90.0)	10(33.3)
Shade	0	5(16.7)
Water	3(10.0)	4(13.3)
Shade and Water	0	11(36.6)
Total	30(100)	30(100)

Figures in brackets indicates percentage

In Kivli, only two persons out of thirty come from a distance which is beyond 5 km. In such case, extra wage of 10 per cent are payable to the workers. They said that they were not aware about such provisions. The mate who was present at the worksite was also unaware about such policy. A large percent of the total workers responded that there is no worksite facilities provided. The workers carry their own water at the worksite. It was found during the visit that there was no worksite facility at the worksite. It has been found that there has been incidence of worker getting injured at the worksite. No medical aid was provided and the worker was taken to the health centre of the village.The workers in Jhadoli are provided work within a radius of 5 km. The response of the respondents regarding the facilities provided at the worksite varies. Some of the respondents said there is nothing at the worksite whereas others told that shade and water was provided at the worksite. Yet, in both the gram panchayat, no crèche facility was provided despite the fact that the women folk bring their young kids at the worksite.

Overall Observation

The overall impact of MGNREGA on the lives of rural households seems to be positive. There were families who did not get a square meal a day. The wage from MGNREGA helped them to have sufficient food. It was found that there are households with good economic conditions and government employees working under MGNREGA scheme. This blocks the work of needy household as there are limited works which are generated. Most of the population here are called *adivasis* under the ST category. This tribal population are dependent on work provided within their villages. They want work under MGNREGA to be provided for more number of days.The *gram sevaks* are actively working for the implementation of the Act. It is the *gram sevaks* who carry out the day to day affair of implementing the policy. The *sarpanch* and *panchayat* secretary were not much aware about the progress of implementation in the *gram panchayats*. They are nominal authorities and concerned with signing and allocation of funds. In this regard, it is worth mentioning that *gram sevaks* were not trained properly which could have improved their capacity in implementing the Act. The *gram sevaks* also complained that their salary is very less as compared to their work. They work for seven days a week and are paid very less salary. Their salary is paid after long intervals which de-motivate them to work. They suggested that their payment should be increased and made on time. They also suggested that strict monitoring by the officials involved in the implementation of the Act is required.

Udaipur

Udaipur district is situated in the southern tip of Rajasthan adjoining Gujarat and is oval in shape with a very narrow strip stretching towards the north. It is located between 2323°46' and 25°5' North Latitude and between 73°9' and 74°35' East Longitude. It bound in the north by Rajsamand and Pali districts, in the south by Dungarpur and Banswara, and Chittaurgarh and Bhilwara districts on the east. The city of Ahmedabad is 250 km on the northeast.

Figure 4.11: Map of Udaipur

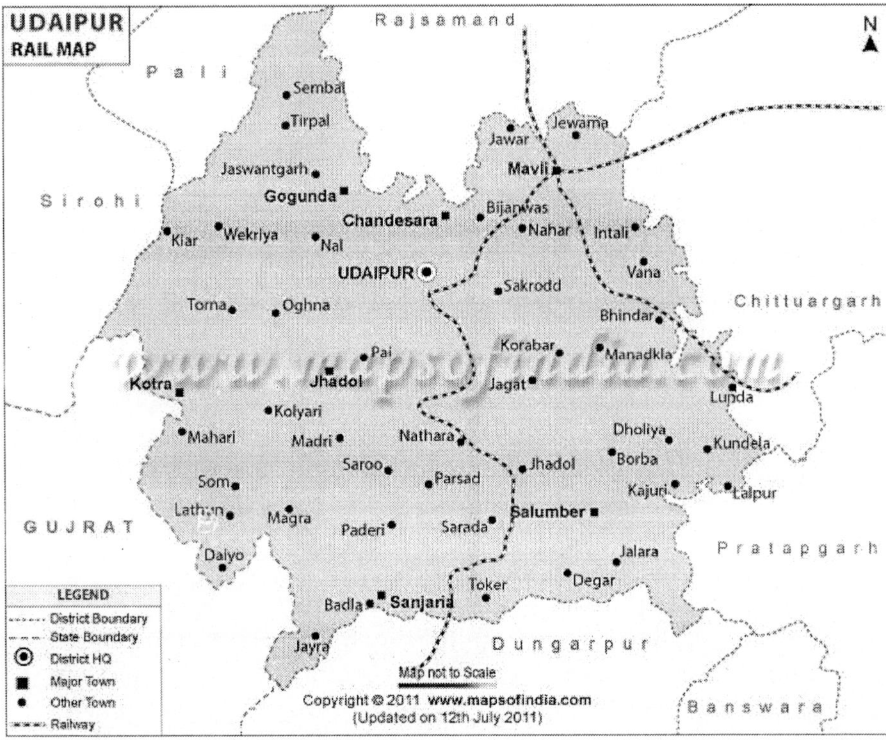

Source: www.mapsofindia.com

Udaipur is a historic capital of the kingdom of Mewar in the former Rajputana agency. The Guhils (Sisodia) clan ruled the Mewar and its capital were shifted from Chittorgarh to Udaipur after founding city of Udaipur by Maharana Uday Singh. The Mewar province became part of Rajasthan after India became independent.

Apart from its history, culture, and scenic locations, it is also known for its Rajput-era palaces. The Lake Palace, for instance, covers an entire island in the Pichola Lake. Many of the palaces have been converted into luxury hotels. It is often called the "Venice of the East", and is also nicknamed the "Lake City". Lake Pichola, Fateh Sagar Lake, Udai Sagar and Swaroop Sagar in this city are considered some of the most beautiful lakes in the state. In context of Rajasthan, Udaipur is the second most-sought after tourist destination of the state, the first being Jaipur. Udaipur had been the capital of Mewar for centuries. Udaipur is an extremely popular destination for travellers due to its mythical architecture, green forests, and renowned lake views. Unfortunately, the city's wealth is held by a sliver of the population, and the vast majority of the local population suffers from a severe lack of supporting infrastructure.

Maharana Udai Singh founded Udaipur in 1559 A.D. According to a legend Udai Singh was guided by a holy man meditating on the hill near Pichola Lake to establish his capital on that very spot. This place was less vulnerable to external invasion than Chittaurgarh because it is surrounded by Aravali Ranges, forests and lakes. Maharana Udai Singh died in 1572 and was succeeded by Maharana Pratap who valiantly defended Udaipur from Mughal attacks. Maharana Pratap is the most revered Rajput icon who gallantly fount the Mughals at the battle of Haldighati in 1576. Mewar continuously defied foreign invaders and has a history of bloody battles until the British intervention in the nineteenth century when a treaty was signed to protect Udaipur. Upon independence, Udaipur merged with the Union of India.

District Profile of Udaipur

The population of Udaipur in 2011 is 3,067,549 of which male and female were 1,566,781 and 1,500,768 respectively. The census in 2001 showed the population of Udaipur as 2,480,657 which include the male and female population of 1,259,170 and 1,221,487 respectively. The population of Udaipur district constitute 4.47 percent of total population of Rajasthan. The figure of the same in 2001 is 4.39 percent of the population of Rajasthan. In census 2001, Udaipur district recorded an increase of 24.27 percent to its population compared to 1991.

Table 4.25 : Demographic Profile of Udaipur District

Description	2011	2001
Population	30,67,549	24,80,657
Male	15,66,781	12,59,170
Female	15,00,768	12,21,487
Population Growth	23.66%	24.27%
Area Sq. Km	12,666	12,666
Density/km2	242	196
Proportion to Rajasthan Population	4.47%	4.39%
Average Literacy (%)	62.74	59.77
Male Literacy	75.91	74.66
Female Literacy	49.1	44.49
Rural-Urban Population in 2011	Rural	Urban
Population (%)	80.15%	19.85%
Total Population	24,58,658	6,08,891
Male Population	12,50,880	3,15,901
Female Population	12,07,778	2,92,990

In 2011, there was change of 23.66 percent in the population compared to population in 2001. The provisional data of Census 2011 shows that density of Udaipur district is 242 people per sq.km. The density in 2001 is 196 people per sq.km.

The literacy rate in 2001 was 59.77 percent which increased to 62.74 percent in 2011. According to Census 2001, the male and female literacy was 74.66 percent and 44.49 percent. In 2011, there was a slight increase in the literacy rate among male and female 75.91 and 49.10 respectively.

Out of the total population as per census 2011 in Udaipur, 80.15 percent lives in rural areas of villages. The total population living in rural areas is 2,458,658 of which males and females are 1,250,880 and 1,207,778 respectively. According to census 2011, the urban population is 608,891 people including 315,901 males and 292,990 females. Out of the total population of the district, 19.85 live in urban regions of the district

The majority of the population in Udaipur is Scheduled Tribe. As per census 2001, out of the total population 47.86 percent of the population is Scheduled Tribe. The proportion of Scheduled Caste out of the total population is only 6.01 percent.

Implementation of MGNREGA in Udaipur

MGNREGA was enacted with an objective to provide a strong social safety net for the vulnerable groups by providing a fall back employment source when other employment alternatives are scarce or inadequate. It aims to empower the rural poor through the processes of a right based law. It tries to address the causes of chronic poverty by providing employment on works such as drought, deforestation and soil erosion. The Act seeks to strengthen the natural resource base of rural livelihood and create durable assets in rural areas. The real potential of MGNREGA to change the face of rural poverty lies in its effective implementation.

Udaipur like the other three districts was selected for implementation of the Act in the first phase. Udaipur region of southern Rajasthan is mostly hilly, with large parts of the hills now being barren. The natural resource base is highly degraded consisting of agricultural lands and forests, pasturelands and wastelands. Due to the inadequacy of the natural resource base in providing ample livelihood options, most families engage in physical labour outside their villages. The numbers of workers in agriculture have decreased most of which have performed badly in agriculture due to recurrent droughts during the late nineties. According to the human development index scale, Udaipur has a low human development[10]. Udaipur was an apt district for the implementation of the Act in the initial phase.

Figure 4.12: Sample of Udaipur District

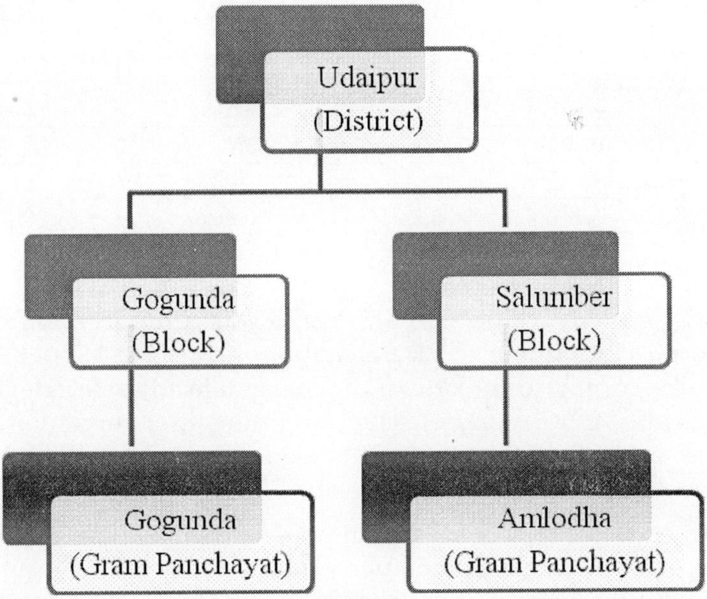

As has been discussed earlier, the two blocks of Udaipur, Gogunda and Salumber were selected using purposive sampling method. The selection of *gram panchayat* in each of the block was done using snowball sampling technique. Using the snowball method, Gogunda *gram panchayat* was selected in Gogunda block and Amlodha *gram panchayat* in Salumber block. In total 60 people were interviewed which includes 30 people in each of the *gram panchayats.*

During the field work, there was no work carried out in both the *gram panchayats.* So the interview of the beneficiaries was conducted in the villages of the *gram panchayats.*

Sample Respondents

In both the *gram panchayats* it is the female of the family who goes to work. When the interview was conducted it was either the head of the household or male member of the family who responded.

Table 4.26 Sample of Respondents in Udaipur

Caste	Male	Female	Total
Gogunda			
SC	0	13(43.3)	13(43.3)
ST	1(3.3)	1(3.3)	2(6.7)
OBC	3(10.0)	12(40.0)	15(50.0)
Total	4 (13.3)	26(86.6)	30(100)
Amlodha			
SC	6(20.0)	2(6.7)	8(26.6)
ST	2(6.7)	3(10.0)	5(16.7)
OBC	2(6.7)	13(43.3)	15(50.0)
General	0	2(6.7)	2(6.7)
Total	10(33.3)	20(66.6)	30(100)

Figures in bracket indicates percentage

The male work participation is low as compared to females in Gogunda. The female work participation rate is 86.7 percent. The workforce comprises mostly of the marginalised caste category with 50 percent of OBC workers. The remaining 43.3 percent is from SC category and 6.7 percent from ST category. This shows that the policy is reaching the targeted population.

In Amlodha, one-third of the population is male while female participation is more than 60 percent. Similarly with Gogunda, half of the sample workers are from OBC category. Workers from SC category are 26.6 percent and ST category is 16.7 percent.

Household Size

The number of household members plays a significant role in MGNREGA. The employment under the Act is guaranteed to a household and not to individual. The less the number of household the income is more beneficial.

The average number of household members in Gogunda is 5-6. There are very few people who have a family of two members. Only one person out of thirty has a family of more than ten members.

The size of a household is Amlodha is almost similar to Gogunda and 3.3 percent have family members of 9-10 and above. The average size of a family household in Amlodha is similar to Gogunda i.e. 5-6 members.

Table 4.27: Household Size of Respondents in Udaipur

No. of Household members	Frequency	Percent	Cumulative Percent
Gogunda			
1-2	3	10.0	10.0
3-4	9	30.0	40.0
5-6	10	33.3	73.3
7-8	7	23.3	96.7
10 & above	1	3.3	100.0
Total	30	100	
Amlodha			
1-2	1	3.3	3.3
3-4	6	20.0	23.3
5-6	18	60.0	83.3
7-8	3	10.0	93.3
9-10	1	3.3	96.7
10 & above	1	3.3	100.0
Total	30	100.0	

Profile of the Sample Respondents

There were not many variations among the workers who have been interviewed in Gogunda. The background of the sample workers were more or less the same. The sample workers in Amlodha have a varied background. There are workers who are entirely dependent on MGNREGA wage for their income as well those who earn more than Rs. 4000 a month from other source. The profile of the sample respondent will enable us to assess the impact of the Act on their lives.

When we look at the above table, it shows that the economic status of the workers is not good. Yet, none of the sample workers in Gogunda have a BPL card. Most of the workers have a land holding of 1-5 Bigha. The proportion of landless worker is 13.3 percent. The average monthly household income is Rs. 2000-2500. Out of the total population, 20 percent are dependent on MGNREGA income for their livelihood.

In Amlodha, out of the total respondents, twenty people have a BPL card. The average household income of the workers is Rs. 1000-1500 in a month. There are very few beneficiaries who are completely dependent on MGNREGA for their income. Only 6.6 percent of the population are dependent on MGNREGA wage while the rest of the population have their own source of income for their livelihood, since the duration of employment provided under the policy is not sufficient to meet the expense of a household. All the workers have their own landholding which is a source of income for many of them.

Table 4.28 : Profile of Sample Respondents in Udaipur

Household Income(Monthly)	BPL card holder	Land Holding			Total
		Landless	1-5 Bigha	6-10 Bigha	
Gogunda					
Only MGNREGA	No	4(13.3)	2(6.7)	0	6(20.0)
1000-1500	No	0	4(13.3)	0	4(13.3)
1500-2000	No	0	1(3.3)	0	1(3.3)
2000-2500	No	0	8(26.7)	0	8(26.7)
2500-3000	No	0	5(16.7)	0	5(16.7)
3000-3500	No	0	5(16.7)	1(3.3)	6(20.0)
Total	No	4(13.3)	25(83.3)	1(3.3)	30(100)

Amlodha

Household Income(Monthly)	BPL card holder	Land Holding		Total
		1-5 Bigha	6-10 Bigha	
Only MGNREGA	Yes	1(3.3)	0	1(3.3)
	No	1(3.3)	0	1(3.3)
1000-1500	Yes	9(30.0)	0	9(30.0)
	No	2(6.7)	0	2(6.7)
2000-2500	Yes	5(16.7)	0	5(16.7)
	No	3(10.0)	0	3(10.0)
3000-3500	Yes	2(6.7)	0	2(6.7)
	No	2(6.7)	0	2(6.7)
3500-4000	Yes	1(3.3)	0	1(3.3)
	No	1(3.3)	0	1(3.3)
4000 & Above	Yes	2(6.7)	0	2(6.7)
	No	0	1(3.3)	1(3.3)
Total		29(96.6)	1(3.3)	30(100)

Figures in bracket indicates percentage

Table 4.29: Awareness Among the Respondents About the Provisions of the Act in Udaipur

Education Qualification	Gram Sabha held			Source of Information about the Act		Signed Receipt after applying for Job		Unemployment Allowance	
	Yes	No	No Idea	Villagers	Panchayat members	Yes	No	Yes	No
Gogunda									
Illiterate	10 (33.3)	9 (30.0)	9 (30.0)	4 (13.3)	24 (80.0)	0	28 (93.3)	0	28 (93.3)
I-V	0	0	1 (3.3)	0	1 (3.3)	0	1 (3.3)	0	1 (3.3)
VI-VIII	0	0	1 (3.3)	0	1 (3.3)	0	1 (3.3)	0	1 (3.3)
Total	10 (33.3)	9 (30.0)	11 (36.6)	4 (13.3)	26 (86.6)	0	30 (100)	0	30 (100)
Amlodha									
Illiterate	7 (23.3)	7 (23.3)	2 (6.7)	1 (3.3)	15 (50.0)	0	16 (53.3)	0	16 (53.3)
1-V	2 (6.7)	5 (16.7)	2 (6.7)	4 (13.3)	5 (16.7)	0	9 (30.0)	0	9 (30.0)
VI-VIII	1 (3.3)	0	1 (3.3)	0	2 (6.7)	1 (3.3)	1 (3.3)	0	2 (6.7)
Secondary	1 (3.3)	0	1 (3.3)	0	2 (6.7)	0	2 (6.7)	0	2 (6.7)
Graduation & Above	1 (3.3)	0	0	0	1 (3.3)	0	1 (3.3)	0	1 (3.3)
Total	12 (40.0)	12 (40.0)	6 (20.0)	5 (16.7)	25 (83.3)	1 (3.3)	29 (96.6)	0	30 (100)

Figures in bracket indicates percentage

Awareness Level

The awareness among the workers about the detailed provisions of the Act is very low. They were aware about the basic entitlement of 100 days of work under MGNREGA. The table below will discuss the awareness level of the workers about the provisions of the Act.

In Gogunda, 93.3 percent of the total respondents were illiterate. Among the respondents, 33.3 percent people said that the *gram sabha* was held and the remaining people said either no or were not aware about *gram sabha* was held or not. Their source of information about the Act is mostly from the *panchayat* members. No one in Gogunda got a signed receipt for applying for employment nor got an unemployment allowance when work was not provided on time. There was not a single person who was aware about unemployment allowances. One of the factors responsible for the low level of awareness among the workers is their low education level. Since most of them are illiterate, they follow with whatever the *panchayat* functionaries make them understand.

The condition in Amlodha is not very different from Gogunda. In response to the question on whether *gram sabha* was held or not, 40 percent said that it was held while 40 percent responded negatively. The rest 20 percent were unaware about *gram sabhas*. As compared to Gogunda, the illiterate population in Amlodha is low that is 53.3 percent. Majority of the people got the information about the Act from *panchayat* members. Only 16.7 percent got to know about the policy from the villagers. A whopping 96.6 percent did not get a signed receipt after applying for job. The signed receipt with date will entitle them to unemployment allowance in case they are not provided job within 15 days. On the other hand, none of them were aware of the provisions of unemployment allowance to request for it.

Duration of Getting a Job Card and Job after Applying

Job card is given to the entire rural household after due verification of place of residence and age of member or members who are adult. The registered households are issued a Job Card with photographs. The Job Card with a unique identification number is the basis for demanding employment. Job card should be provided within 15 days of registration and similar employment should be provided within 15 days of application. The following Table 3.30 will give a glimpse of the duration of issuing a job and providing employment on demand.

Table 4.30 : Duration of Getting Job Card and Job after Applying in Udaipur

Days	Gogunda		Amlodha	
	Duration of getting JC	On Demand-Job Duration	Duration of getting JC	On Demand-Job Duration
10-15 Days	7(23.3)	4(13.3)	0	0
15-20 Days	1(3.3)	0	6(20.0)	7(23.3)
20-25 Days	0	0	5(16.7)	0
30 & above	22(73.3)	26(86.7)	19(63.3)	23(76.7)
Total	30(100)	30(100)	30(100)	30(100)

Figures in bracket indicates percentage

In Gogunda, 23.3 percent of the beneficiaries got a job card on time but 73.3 percent got a job card after 30 days and more. Job was provided on time to only 13.3 percent of the total population. The remaining 86.7 percent got a job only after 30 and above days.

The majority of the people in Amlodha got a job card after 30 and above days. Out of the total, 20.0 got a job card within 15-20 days while 16.7 percent got it within 20-25 days. 76.7 percent of the total respondents got a job after a month and above while 23.3 percent got it within 15-20 days.

Number of Days Worked by the respondents in the Financial Year 2010-11

The Act guarantees right to work for 100 days to a household in a financial year. The performance of the Act can be looked at from this basic commitment of the state towards the rural poor. The graph below shows the number of days a person has worked under the scheme in a financial year.

Figure 4.13: No of Days worked by the respondents in financial year 2010-11 in Udaipur

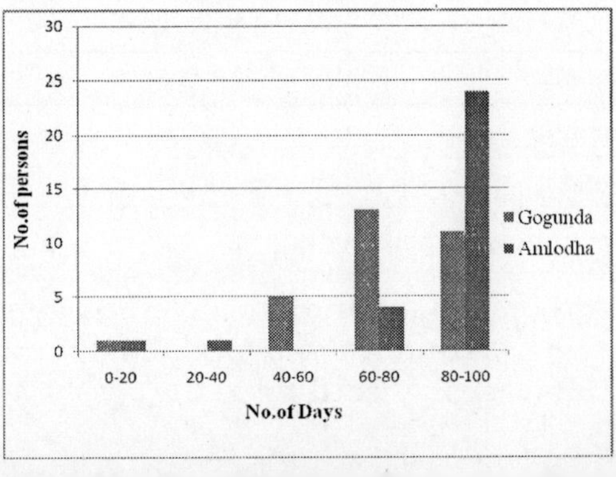

A large number of people in Gogunda have worked for 60-80 days only. More than half of the total sample did not complete the stipulated 100 days of employment.

In Amlodha, a large percentage of the population have worked for 80-100 days under MGNREGA in the financial year 2010-11. As we have seen that most of the workforce are women. So many of them are engaged in household work which deter them to complete the 100 day cycle of employment. Being the home maker of the household, their commitment towards their family and children is high. Working at MGNREGA is of less importance as compared to their household work. They work in MGNREGA only to supplement their family income.

Payment Related Issues

The main gap in the implementation of MGNREGA is found in the payments made to the workers. Usually workers are not paid their wage within 15 days which is the maximum time limit. There are also discrepancies in the amount paid to the workers. The following tabulation of the responses from the workers will give a fair idea about the issues related with payments made to the workers.

Table 4.31: Payment Related Issues in Udaipur

Gram Panchayat	Gogunda	Amlodha
Payment received per day (in Rs.)		
60-70	0	6(20.0)
70-80	0	13(43.3)
80-90	30(100)	4(13.3)
90-100	0	3(10.0)
100 & above	0	4(13.3)
Total	30(100)	30(100)
Frequency of Payment		
15 days-1 month	4(13.3)	9(30.0)
1-2 months	19(63.3)	21(70.0)
2-3 months	7(23.3)	0
Total	30(100)	30(100)

Figures in bracket indicates percentage

All the workers in Gogunda received a payment between Rs. 80-90 in a day. In Gogunda, the people complained that they are not paid their full wages. According to the *panchayat,* wages are paid according to the measurement of their work done. The *panchayat* members said that workers which consist mostly of female workers cannot complete their task so they are paid less. The frequency of payment varies between 15 days to 2-3 months time. Mostly the payments are made in 1-2 months time. Men and women are paid wages equally. There is no discrimination on the basis of gender.

The wage received in Amlodha starts from Rs. 60 which is less than the minimum wage. The statutory minimum wage in Rajasthan is Rs. 73. The average wage rate is Rs. 70-80 per day. The maximum amount received per day is Rs. 100-110. The workers get their payment mostly after a month's time. There are few (30.0%) people who said that they receive their payments between 15- 30 days time. Payments are made either through post office or bank. The respondents said that payment made through cash was more convenient for them. They get cash in hand whereas getting payment through bank and post office is a hassle for them.

Worksite Related Issues

Under the Act, it should be ensured that worksite facilities should be provided which includes shade, drinking water and crèche at all the worksites. Since there was no work going on at the time of data collection in Udaipur, the first hand observation of the worksite could not be done. The below table 3.32 represents the response of the workers who were interviewed in the village.

Table 4.32 : Worksite Related Issues in Udaipur

Gram Panchayats	Gogunda	Amlodha
Distance of worksite (in km.)		
1 km	5(16.7)	5(16.7)
2 km	6(20.0)	5(16.7)
3 km	6(20.0)	6(20.0)
4 km	6(20.0)	5(16.7)
5 km	5(16.7)	7(23.3)
6 km	2(6.7)	1(3.3)
7 km	0	1(3.3)
Total	30(100)	30(100)
Worksite Facilities		
Nothing	0	6(20.0)
Shade	11(36.7)	9(30.0)
Water	10(33.3)	9(30.0)
Water and Shade	9(30.0)	6(20.0)
Total	30(100)	30(100)

Figures in bracket indicates percentage

Most of the workers in Gogunda are provided work within the radius of 5 km except for two people. The two respondents are entitled for an extra wage of 10 percent for transportation. But because of their lack of awareness, they did not get any such allowances. According to the respondents, there was some facility or the other provided at the worksite.

Similar with Gogunda, only two people in Amlodha comes from a distance which is beyond 5 km from their place of residence. They were also not given any extra allowances as in the case of people in Gogunda. There was variation in the response of the workers regarding worksite facilities. Some 20 percent of them said that nothing is provided at the worksite while the remaining people said only shade and water are provided. While the rest 20 percent said that both water and shade were provided. There was no medical aid provided at the worksite which is necessary as there are incidences of workers getting injured.

Overall Observation

In Udaipur, the impact of MGNREGA varies. The implementation in Amlodha is found to be more efficient as compared to Gogunda. For the poor rural household the Act is very significant. But because of loopholes in the Act, the Act doesn't have a strong impact. The Act is only an additional income for the rural poor. In Udaipur, migration still continues.

The impact on the lives of rural women is significant to some extent. Although the women do not have access to their own income from MGNREGA, their status in the family has improved. It was found that domestic violence in the family has reduced. The real sense of empowerment still remains a distant dream. The *panchayat* functionaries are actively working for the implementation of the Act.

The situation in matter of payment is not different in Udaipur. There are delays in the payment of wages. The only factor which seems to be responsible for such delay is lack of coordination among the PRIs and government officials. Due to this, there is inadequate work to fulfil the demand for work by the beneficiaries.

Endnotes

1 Bhils are a group of tribal community

2 Government of Rajasthan and Institute of Development Studies(2009) "Dungarpur District Human Development Report,2009"; A Study Conducted by the Institute of Development Studies, Jaipur for the Government of Rajasthan and Planning Commission of India.

3 Government of India (2003) "Report of the Task Force on: Identification of Districts for Wage and Self Employment Programmes"; Planning Commission, Government of India.

4 Originally Statistical Package for the Social Sciences later modified as Statistical Product and Service Solutions. Now it is officially known as IBM SPSS Statistics.

5 The details of the productivity norms are listed in the Schedule of Rates (SoRs). The SoRs are calculated through Work Time and Motion Studies. The SoRs, under the Act, have to be such that an average person working for nine hours, with one hour of rest, is able to earn the notified MGMGNREGA minimum wage.

6 Exceptions are made if the State Government has an exemption from the Government of India (GoI), specifying a plausible reason.

7 Government of Rajasthan and Institute of Development Studies(2009) "Jhalawar District Human Development Report,2009"; A Study Conducted by the Institute of Development Studies, Jaipur for the Government of Rajasthan and Planning Commission of India.

8 Government of India (2003) "Report of the Task Force on: Identification of Districts for Wage and Self Employment Programmes"; Planning Commission, Government of India.

9 James Tod,(1839) "Travels in Western India"; W.H. Allen and Company, London.

10 Government of Rajasthan and Institute of Development Studies(2008) "Human Development Report Rajasthan: An Update-2008"; A Study Conducted by the Institute of Development Studies, Jaipur for the Government of Rajasthan and Planning Commission of India in GoI and UNDP assisted project "Strengthening State Plans for Human Development".

5

A Comparison of the Four Districts

The concept of right to work under MGNREGA is to provide guaranteed employment on demand to all the sections of society in rural areas. MGNREGA is a national Act which has to be implemented uniformly in all the rural areas covered under the Act. The study was conducted in the four districts i.e. Dungarpur, Jhalawar, Sirohi and Udaipur of Rajasthan in order to assess the implementation of the Act. A comparative analysis of the findings from the four districts will help to look at the intrastate variations in the level and quality of implementation within a state. It will enable us to identify the loopholes and see how they can be addressed. Similarly, the success stories of its implementation can be identified and used as an example for others in the implementation of the Act.

The performance of implementing MGNREGA in Rajasthan shows a varied picture. There are various studies which reveal that Rajasthan is one of the best performing states in India. There are also stories of drawbacks and loopholes in the implementation of the Act. This chapter will draw comparisons on the implementation of the Act in the four districts based on the analysis of the findings discussed in the previous chapter. The main provisions which are meant for effective implementation of the Act are discussed below.

Basic Entitlements for the Beneficiaries

The basic entitlement under the MGNREGA is to provide 100 days of work to a rural household on demand. It will ensure that livelihood security is provided through employment opportunities.

The policy mandates a minimum wage which means the minimum wage fixed by the State Government under section 3 of the Minimum Wages Act 1948 for agricultural laborers. The wage should be paid equally to both men and women. The policy is implemented in a bottom-up manner with a self-selecting and demand driven approach. It is a right based programme where provision of work is triggered by demand for work by the rural poor.

Demand for Job Card

The Act states that any registered rural household should be issued a Job Card(JC) by the *gram panchayat*. The JC should be issued within a fortnight of the application for registration after verification. The timely issue of a well designed JC is essential and it should be issued in the presence of the local community. It is a critical legal document which also helps to ensure transparency and protect laborers against fraud. The JC should be in the custody of the household to whom it is issued.

In all the four districts, majority of the households got a JC after 30 days of registration. Except for Sirohi, a small proportion of people in Dungarpur (10.0%), Jhalawar (10.0%) and Udaipur (11.6%) got a JC within 10-15 days of registering. Many of the respondents in Sirohi and Udaipur were found without a JC. According to the respondents, JC is not required anymore after the payments are made through banks and post offices. Some of them have lost their JC and others have submitted to the *panchayat* members. The *panchayat* members on enquiry responded that the entry for wage is mentioned in the pass book provided by banks and post offices. They said that they keep the JC because it is convenient for them to prepare muster roll and allocate work in a rotational manner. This is a violation of the Act. In case of Jhalawar and Dungarpur, they have the JC with them but there was no account of work provided and wages paid to the households were recorded. The condition of JC of most of the respondents in Jhalawar was in a dilapidated condition (shown in picture). There were discrepancies in the names entered in the JC. The photograph of all the adult household members was not there in many of the JC. Comparatively the JC of beneficiaries in Dungarpur was found to be in a better condition and without discrepancies. The cost of photograph for JC was paid for by the households in all the districts. Although it was to be provided free of cost.

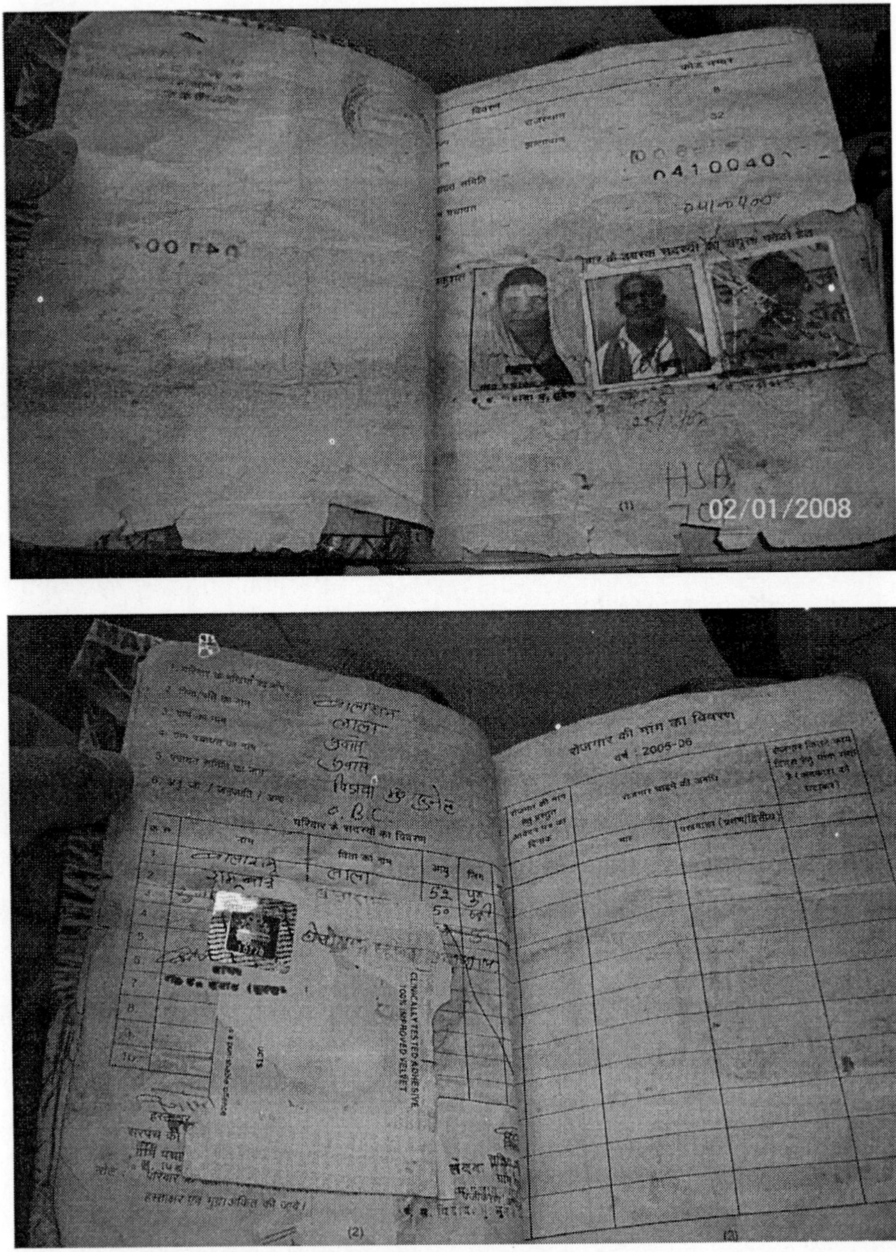

Picture 5.1: Condition of Job Card in Jhalawar District

Demand for Work

Households with a JC are eligible to apply for a job. A written application is to be made to the *gram panchayat* seeking for job mentioning the duration and time for which work is sought. A dated receipt of the application for employment should be provided by the *gram panchayat.* The dated receipt will guarantee employment within 15 days. In case employment is not provided within 15 days an unemployment allowance is to be paid by the state government. The Act is designed to offer an incentive structure to the states by providing employment as ninety percent of the cost for employment provided is borne by the Centre. There is a concomitant disincentive for not providing employment as the states then bear the double indemnity of unemployment and the cost of unemployment allowance. Yet, there was violation of such provisions which are essential for effective implementation of the Act.

We have seen in the previous chapter that many of the households are dependent entirely on the income from MGNREGA. For others, MGNREGA income is an additional income for the rural households and fall back option particularly during the lean season. Dutta et.al. has also pointed out that there are a number of distinct ways in which MGMGNREGA is likely to impact poverty, the most direct and obvious way is by providing extra work opportunities and income to the poorest in the rural areas[1].

It was found that in Jhalawar and Udaipur, a small percentage of the respondents were provided employment within 15 days of applying for a job. In Jhalawar, the percentage was 15 and the same in Udaipur was 6.6 percent. Majority of the respondents in all the four districts were provided work after 30 days of demand for job. The common phenomenon which appeared in all the four districts was lack of enough work to address the demands of the beneficiaries. While the essence of the Act is its demand driven approach but work are not provided on demand. The *panchayat* functionaries stated that there is not enough work to meet the increasing demand of the rural poor. It was found in Jhalawar that since there is inadequate work, the *panchayat* members provide work in a rotational manner. It ensures that households demanding work are provided for even if it means less than 100 days.

No. of Days Worked

The MGNREGA is to provide for the enhancement of livelihood security of the households in rural areas of the country by providing at least one hundred days of guaranteed wage employment in every financial year to every rural household whose adult members volunteer to do unskilled manual work.

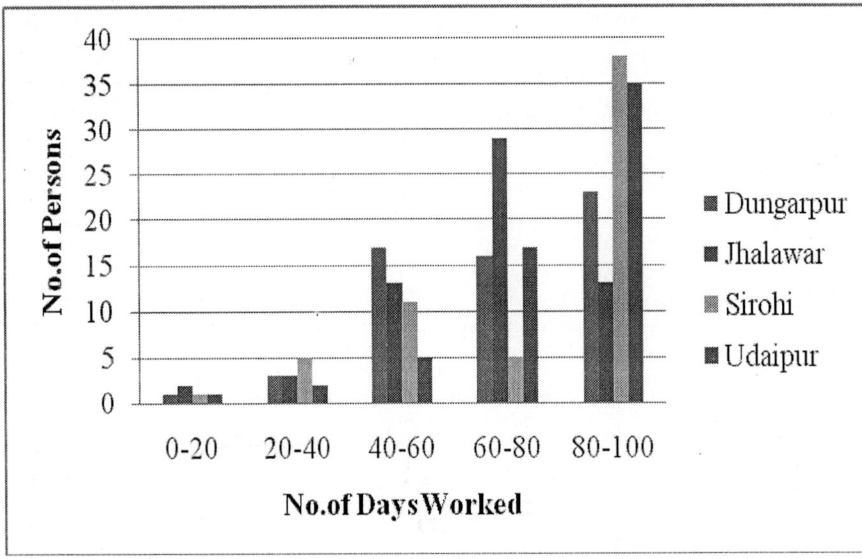

Figure 5.1: A Comparison of No. of Days Worked by the Respondents in Financial Year 2010-11

When we look at the above figure, it shows that Sirohi has provided 80-100 days to a maximum number of people. It was also found that people have access to work on demand. Next to Sirohi it is Udaipur which provided maximum days of work to thirty-five people out of sixty. Here many of the respondents completed 100 days of employment in the financial year 2010-11. The findings of Udaipur also show that workers who have completed 100 days of employment are those who are totally dependent on MGNREGA income for their livelihood. This shows that the poor households have been benefitted from the employment provided by the policy. The credit for providing constant work in Udaipur and Sirohi goes to the block level officials and the panchayat functionaries who are actively involved in creating works. The interview with the officials and panchayat functionaries show their commitment towards the implementation of the Act. There is a well coordinated effort between the officials and the panchayat functionaries. The workers in Udaipur are provided work in other departments like forest and agriculture. Similarly in Sirohi, work is provided in construction of *panchayat bhavan* and other government buildings. The two districts are making an effort to provide at least the basic employment of 100 days.

Picture 5.2: Construction of *Panchayat Bhavan* in Sirohi

The beneficiaries reveal that many of them are willing to work for more than 100 days a year particulary those workers who are completely dependent on MGNREGA income. Many sections of the society have been trying to pressurize the government to increase the days of guaranteed employment to 200 days in a financial year. The income from MGNREGA is of great significance for the rural poor. Yet, the guaranteed 100 days of work is not provided to the workers on demand. The issue which arises is the sustainability of the Act. Whether the Act will continue to provide guaranteed work on demand is the big question.

Wage Payment

The wages are paid as per the State-wise Government of India (GoI) notified MGNREGA wages. It is paid according to piece rate as the Schedule of Rates (SoRs). The SoRs are calculated through Work Time and Motion Studies. The SoRs, under the Act, have to be such that an average person working for nine hours, with one hour of rest, is able to earn the notified MGNREGA minimum wage. Payment of wages is mandatorily done through the individual/joint bank/post office beneficiary accounts.

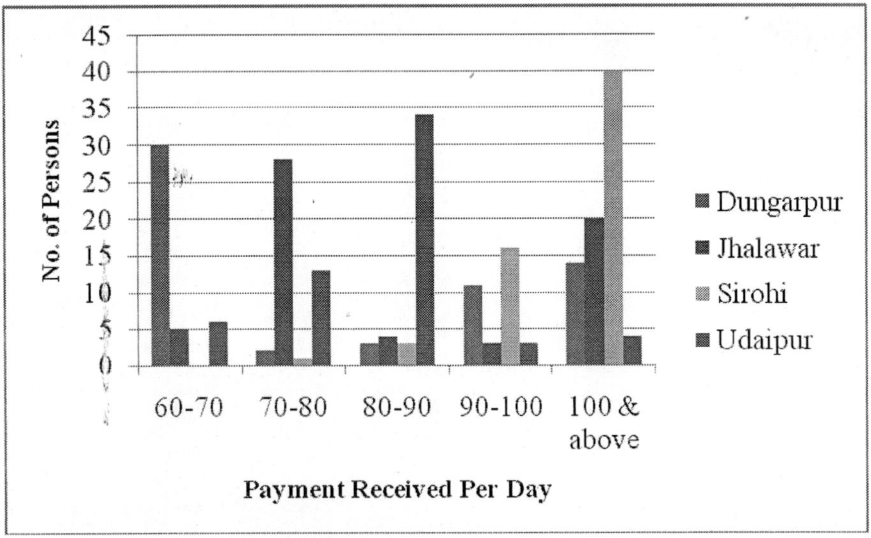

Figure 5.2: Comparison of Payment Received Per Day (in Rs.)

Among the four districts, Sirohi has given the maximum wage payment to the beneficiaries. The minimum wage in Sirohi is Rs.70-80 per day. The minimum wage in rest of the four districts is Rs.60-70. Majority of the population in Dungarpur got payment of Rs. 60-70 per day. The same in Jhalawar is Rs.70-80 per day and Udaipur is Rs.80-90. The above figure shows that the implementation in Sirohi is more effective than the other three districts. The maximum wage is provided to the workers which can be a significant income for their livelihood. In November, 2010 the government of Rajasthan agreed to the agitating demand of workers led by Mazdoor Kisan Shakti Sanghatan to increase the wage rate of MGNREGA workers[2]. The rate under the MGNREGA scheme for specified work in eight hours is Rs. 100 per day. Yet the workers are paid less wage.

The main flaws in the implementation of the policy appears in the wage rate and payment made to the beneficiaries. There are reports of corruption in the implementation of the Act which is mostly related with discrepancies in wage disbursement and utilisation. Many of the beneficiaries' complaint of non payment of stipulated wage has been of great concern in the implementation of the Act. It was found that most of the beneficiaries who are illiterate were unable to calculate their wage and the days for which they have worked. The mate who usually prepares the muster roll and wages to be paid takes the benefit and pay less wage to them. This is also one of the reasons for people not being entirely dependent on income from

MGNREGA. It was also seen that many people are losing hope in this pro-poor policy because of its delayed payment and low wage rate. According to the *panchayat* members, wages are paid according to the work done. Since most of the workers are female, they are unable to complete their task so they are paid accordingly. This kind of situation was more prevalent in Jhalawar and Dungarpur.

Another pertinent issue was the payment through banks. Many of the beneficiaries who are landless had problem in opening bank accounts. Without a bank account they were not given work on the pretext that payment will made only through banks. The other issue was access to banks which are usually located in far off places. Most of the respondents complained that often they travel to far off banks only to find that their payment has not been credited in their account. They said that they do not get the benefits of MGNREGA income when they need it. They also demanded that wages should be increased according to the inflation rate.

Frequency of Payment and other related Issues

According to the Act, payment of wages has to be done on a weekly basis and not beyond a fortnight in any case. There is clear violation of the Act in all the four districts. Delay in payment is one of the most common flaws of the Act. There are households who rely on MGNREGA income for their livelihood income. For them delay in payments affect their daily bread.

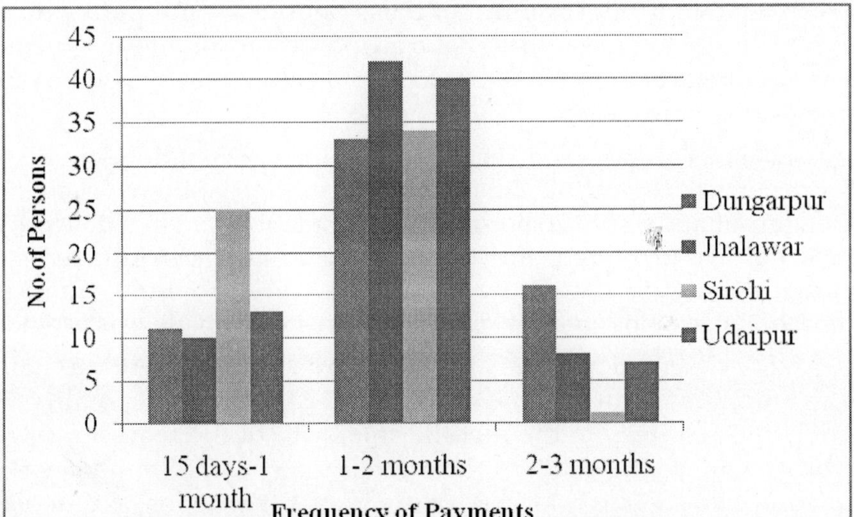

Figure 5.3: Comparison of Frequency of Payments

The above Figure 5.2 shows that the average payment time in all the districts is 1-2 months. As compared to other districts, Sirohi is in a better position by disbursing payment within 15 days-1 month time. In Jhalawar, people have reported that the payments of beneficiaries are due for nearly three months. Delay in payment has been a common phenomenon in all the districts. The officials claim that the delay is caused by higher authorities who do not disburse funds on time. Similarly, the panchayat members blame the officials for delay in the payment. The officials said that the panchayat functionaries do not send the development plan on time to get it approved which gets the whole process delayed.

Worksite Facilities

Under the provision of the Act, work should be provided within 5 km radius of the village. An extra wage of 10 percent is payable to those workers who are coming from a distance beyond 5 km. The Act also prohibits the use of contractors or machinery in execution of the works to ensure that the workers are benefitted directly under the scheme. The worksite facilities which need to be provided include worksite facilities such as crèche, drinking water, first aid medical box, etc. This will ensure that the beneficiaries are provided dignified work.

Majority of the respondents are provided work within 5 km of their residence. There are some people in all the districts who come from a distance which is beyond 5 km. The percentage in Dungarpur is 5 percent, 15 percent in Jhalawar, 2 percent in Sirohi and 6.6 percent in Udaipur. Yet these people are not paid extra 10 percent wage to meet additional transportation and living expenses. The beneficiaries and even the mate in Sirohi were unaware of such provisions in the Act.

There was a mixed response from the respondents in all the four districts regarding the facilities provided at the worksites. In Dungarpur and Sirohi, majority of the population said that no worksite facilities are provided. But in Jhalawar, a large percentage of the respondents said that water and shade were provided. Similarly, most of the respondents in Udaipur said that only shade was provided.

The observation at the worksite also shows that there was hardly any worksite facility. It was also observed that crèche facility was not provided despite the fact that majority of the workforce were women with young children. This deters many of the women workers to complete their work. It is also one of the reasons why women workers are unable to complete the cycle of 100 days of employment in a year.

Awareness Level

The main issue which is plaguing the implementation of MGNREGA is lack of awareness among the beneficiaries. The workers were very much aware of job entitlement for 100 days scheme which they commonly call "Narega" or "Job Card". Yet, the beneficiaries were unaware about the detailed provisions of the Act. MGNREGA is a right based policy. The beneficiaries need to be fully aware of their rights so that they can claim their rights. Awareness level among the beneficiaries is a major factor in the successful implementation of the Act.

The fact lies that awareness level among the beneficiaries is quite low. When we compare the awareness level among the four districts, the awareness level of Sirohi was high followed by Udaipur, Dungarpur and Jhalawar. In Sirohi, maximum number of respondents was aware about *gram sabha* held in the village. A major proportion of people in other districts either said that no *gram sabhas* were held or they had no idea whether it was held or not. Nevertheless, *gram sabhas* are the main decision making and implementing agency in MGNREGA. All the announcements and planning of the Act is done by the *gram sabha*. It is also the duty of the *gram sabha* to conduct social audit of the work taken up by the *gram panchayat*. Many of the respondents do not take active part in the *gram sabhas* held.

In comparison with other three districts, the number of people who got a signed receipt after applying for job was more in Sirohi although the percentage was low with 15 %. Nevertheless, gram sabhas are the main decision making and implementing agency in MGNREGA. All the announcements and planning of the Act is done by the gram sabha. It is also the duty of the *gram sabha* to conduct social audit of the work taken up by the *gram panchayat*.

It is noteworthy that none of the total respondent of 240 was aware of the provision of unemployment allowance. As it has been discussed above, that work is not provided in the stipulated time of 15 days. Despite the fact that there is delay in providing work, beneficiaries are not getting any such allowances. They do not claim for their rights because of their low awareness level. Moreover, they do not get a signed receipt which can entitle them for such provisions.

From the findings, it is clear that most of the beneficiaries were illiterate. The highest illiterate population is in Dungarpur with 98.3 percent. Udaipur and Sirohi has lower illiterate people with 73.3 percent and 81.6 percent respectively. The educational qualifications of the beneficiaries are one of the factors responsible for their awareness about the policy and its entitlements. As we have seen that the awareness level among the people in Sirohi and Udaipur is more than the other two districts, the educational qualification of the people is very significant.

This aspect has been discussed in many other studies as well. A survey conducted by G.B. Pant Social Science Institute, Allahabad in 2008 showed that awareness level among workers was still low. Less than half of the sample workers were aware of their rights. It also highlighted that as most of the rural poor are illiterate, they are not aware of their basic rights which include employment on demand, minimum wages, payment within 15 days and basic worksite facilities[3].

The majority of the population got the information about the Act from the *panchayat* members. It was found that no hoardings, padhyatras, street plays, etc. were held to spread the awareness regarding the Act. Advertisement regarding the Act was put on the walls of panchayat offices. Printed hoardings are of no use to the illiterate population which are in maximum numbers. It is the responsibility of the implementing agencies that the question of awareness among the beneficiaries should be raised.

Impact on Gender

The policy of MGNREGA was designed in a manner to achieve inclusive growth in rural India. It aims to empower the marginalized sections of the society particularly SC, ST and Women. The Act states that "while providing employment, priority shall be given to women in such a way that at least one-third of the beneficiaries shall be women who have registered and requested for work under the Scheme (MGNREGA, Schedule II, Section 6). The encouraging impact of the Act is that large percentage of worker were women in all the four districts. Rajasthan has been one of the states in India with a large percentage of women work participation. As per the Ministry of Rural Development, the work participation rate of women in December, 2012 is 69.2 percent.

From the analysis of findings in the previous chapter, it is clear that the majority of the workforce is women. All the females of the four districts responded that they are paid equal wages except for few old women in Jhalawar. According to the *panchayat* members, old women are unable to work because of their physical health. They hardly complete the task given to them. So, they are paid less wages. It was seen in Sirohi that women were given work according to their capacity. This has enabled the old women folks who have been abandoned by family members to earn their livelihood. The picture below shows that many of the women are elderly women.

The policy has shown that women in rural areas have moved a step forward towards empowerment. Many of the female respondents said that the availability of work within the vicinity of their residence has helped them to work for income. The employment under MGNREGA is considered dignified work by society, since the work is provided by government within the village and a decent wage is paid for work. The women workforce feels that the Act is a providential thing for them. They are now able to contribute to the household income. The income substantiates the household income which is beneficial for the whole family.

The employment of women under MGNREGA has brought social changes in the mindset of the people in rural areas. Women now feel a sense of belongingness to society. The role of women in a family as home-maker and subordinate is changing. Women now take active part in the decision making process in the family. In Udaipur, it was found that domestic violence against women in the family has reduced to a certain extent. Their economic stability has brought a social change in the mindset of the conservative and male dominated society of rural India. The social status of women as subordinates has changed. An encouraging impact of women participation was seen on education specially pre-primary and primary level. As women of the family work under MGNREGA, children of the family are sent to government schools. Government schools also provide mid day meal which makes school the best place to keep their children. Subsequently, there is increase in the number of students enrolled in school.

Yet the fact lies that real sense of empowerment is still a distant dream. The male of the household continue to exploit the women workers. It was seen that women workers were treated in a biased manner by male workers as well as the male mate at the worksite. It was also found that many of the women do not have access to their income. The incomes of the female workers still continue to be with the men of the family. Men usually withdraw the money from bank since the JC is registered in the name of the head of the households. This phenomenon was more prominent in Jhalawar, while the women workforce in Sirohi was more vocal about their rights and was more in control of their income.

"Women Everywhere"

Picture 5.3: Worksites in Dungarpur, Jhalawar and Sirohi.

Impact on Migration

The problem of migration in India has been on the rise particularly internal migration. Internal migration ranges from daily commuting to seasonal migration. Internal migration mostly involves people who are economically poor, less educated and of lower castes. This kind of migration has become a daily strategy of livelihood for people living in marginal areas. Internal migration usually takes place between villages within the same districts, across districts and across states. Migration also takes place to cities and urban areas for better employment opportunities. One of the main aims of MGNREGA was to provide employment opportunity to rural household with the objective to check rural-urban migration. Rural-urban migration has played a significant role in the urbanization process of several countries and continues to be significant in scale, even though migration rates have slowed down in some countries. This rural-urban migration has led to many urban problems like overcrowding and increased population, urban poverty, increase in crime rate, etc. This kind of migration might be beneficial at individual level but it is of net loss to both rural and urban areas leading to a greater regional concentration of wealth, income and human capital may occur.

Although many studies have reported that MGNREGA has able to check migration from rural areas by providing work within the villages (Bhatia,2009[4]; Drèze,2010[5]). It has been observed that the Act has barely any impact on migration in the four districts of Rajasthan. The head (man) of the household still continues to work out of the village. The only transformation is that earlier, the whole household used to migrate but now only the male or earning members of the household continue to work outside the district and state. This has brought some stability in their family lives. The children are getting enrolled in schools. The education of children was earlier considered to be difficult because of their constant movement.

The analysis revealed the reasons for less impact of MGNREGA on migration. Firstly, the amount of wage paid under MGNREGA is less compared to what they earn from their regular work. They earn more from the work in urban areas and cities. Secondly, employment is provided only for 100 days out of 365 days. The limited duration of providing work under the scheme leads to the workers to continue with their jobs which are mostly outside the village. Thirdly, it has been observed that the rural mindset of men being the superior in the family affects the work participation. The men workers considers the work of MGNREGA as work for women and working for a low wage affects the self esteem of men. Fourthly, the income from MGNREGA is not sufficient to accommodate the needs of the family with the increasing price of essential commodities.

Overall Observation

From the above analysis, it shows that the Act has brought changes in the socio economic conditions of many in the rural areas. For a poor household who used to live on one square meal a day the Act is a relief for them and provides them with some basic social security. The fact remains that it is a big leap forward in generation of employment and in the living conditions of the rural poor. It brought a drastic change in the lives of rural people particularly women and the marginalised sections of the society. Rajasthan has been one of the states in India with a large percentage of women work participation. As per the MoRD, the work participation rate of women in December, 2012 is 69.2 per cent. One of the reasons of large percentage of women work participation rate is that their male counterpart prefers to continue with their respective occupations.

One of the positive impacts of MGNREGA is that it has helped women in rural areas to come out of their closed shell. The women respondents said that the enactment of MGNREGA has been a fortunate thing to them. The wage from MGNREGA income is an additional income for the family. It has a social impact as well in the lives of women. In rural areas, mostly women are treated as subordinate in a household. They do not have a say in the family. However, after MGNREGA it has changed their social status. They are taking active part in the decision making of the family.

This bright side does not undermine the fact that many of the PRI functionaries are inactive and they are not aware about their roles in the implementation of MGNREGA. The issue is compounded by the lack of activities for capacity building of PRIs by the bureaucrats in most of the *panchayats*. This shows the lack of responsibility on the part of bureaucrats in the involvement of PRIs in the planning and execution of the policy. In addition, due to lack of educated members in the local bodies, social audit which is to be conducted by the *Gram Sabha* is not conducted in most of the *panchayats* as they are not aware of the provision of social audit in the Act. Moreover, there is no denying the fact that women members are not actively participating in the decision making and implementing of the Act. Lastly, the other intent of the Act was to strengthen the PRI which has still not really happened everywhere. So, the decade old struggle to strengthen this age old institution (*panchayats*) still continues.

Endnotes

1 P.Dutta, R. Murgai, M. Ravallion and M.V. Dominique (2012) "Does India's Employment Guarantee Scheme Guarantee Employment?"; Policy Research Paper, World Bank, Washington D.C.

2 Business Standard (2010) "Rajasthan agrees to MGNREGA workers' demand"; Business Standard, November 18, 2010, New Delhi.

3 Jean Drèze and Reetika Khera (2009) "The Battle for Employment Guarantee"; Frontline , 26 (1):3-16 January,2009

4 Kartika Bhatia (2009) "MGNREGA: A Guarantee against Migration?" mimeo, G.B. Pant Social Science Institute, Allahabad.

5 Jean Drèze (2010) "Employment Guarantee and the Right to Work" in Niraja Gopal Jayal and Pratap Bhanu Mehta (ed.) *Oxford Companion to Indian Politics*; Oxford University Press, New Delhi

6

Conclusion: Observations and Recommendations

The policy of MGNREGA was launched by the government of India with an objective to address the issue of rural poverty by an overarching goal of inclusive growth. The main issue in the implementation of a government policy in India has always been the large discrepancies between the intended and actual implementation of the policy. Whatever the objectives of a policy, it is the implementation which is important. In India, implementation of a policy is of prime importance. The implementation of policies particularly policies related to the welfare of the public has an impact on the survival and continuance of the government. MGNREGA is considered to be a flagship programme of the UPA government. So, its implementation is of utmost importance to the government.

Overall Observations

Among the anti-poverty policies in India in my opinion so far MGNREGA is the best policy. MGNREGA has great potential to revolutionize the rural livelihoods in India. It can generate large employment opportunities and lead to citizen capacity building and thus to an increase in the per capita income. Some of the thrust areas in MGNREGA are discussed below:

India is a signatory to all the employment related human rights covenants, which it is obliged to comply with. Indian Constitution also refers to the right to work under the "directive principles of state policy". Article 39 urges the State to ensure that "the citizens, men and women equally, have the right to an adequate means to livelihood", and that "there is equal pay for equal work for both men and women". Further, Article 41 stresses that "the state, shall within the limits of its economic capacity and development, make effective provision for securing right to work". However, the Indian Constitution did not include the right to work as an enforceable right in the fundamental rights for citizens.

As we know poverty is the consequence of the denial or violation of human rights. MGNREGA enforces a judicially enforceable obligation on the state to provide 100 days of guaranteed employment to every household with a minimum wage. This rights-based approach is indeed a significant breakthrough in the long history of various anti-poverty and wage employment programs undertaken by India since Independence. A right based and legally guaranteed programme is preferred over a state administered programme since it is less bureaucratic. This act has also paved the way for many other such right based Acts. Some of the right based Acts which have come up in the recent years are the Right to Information Act, the Right to Education Act and the Right to Food is in the process of becoming an Act.

The demand driven approach of the policy makes it mandatory for the government to provide work. Work is provided on the basis of self identification of beneficiaries. For the first time in India, such policy brings the role of the state as provider of livelihood within the reach of the beneficiaries. Work should be provided as and when it is most needed. The legal mandate of providing employment in a time bound manner is underpinned by the provision of Unemployment Allowance. It also ensures that the state government is committed towards the realization of the Act by making it to provide an Unemployment Allowance. It is also the largest employment guarantee programme in the world. It is for the first time a universal guarantee of work for the entire rural Indian citizen is provided.

In the Liberalisation, Privatisation and Globalisation (LPG) era, it is the government's largest social security network. This is an era of globalization and everyone is talking about socio economic changes. In India, LPG era is characterized by high economic growth rate but due to liberal policies, there is no employment particularly in the rural areas. So, this era has been termed as an era of jobless growth with decreasing employment rate. Under such circumstances, MGNREGA is trying to address the issue of unemployment in the rural areas where unemployment is highest. India's MGNREGA is the only Act which is giving its rural people such a right that too in this era of LPG. It has a vital role to play because of its humane approach. It serves as an effective safety net for the unemployed especially during famine and drought. It has enabled them with sufficient purchasing power and they are able to at least acquire basic food security. The Act has confined the rural poor in their areas and stopped migration to the cities. It is not only giving rural livelihood but also involving them in other non-agricultural work. This has helped in handling the problem of disguised unemployment as and when needed. Employment in other non-agricultural work will also improve the rural infrastructure i.e. rural asset building, ultimately leading to sustainable development.

MGNREGA gives economic empowerment to the rural poor and such meaningful employment makes them feel that they matter to society. This increases their confidence, which is necessary for social and human development. Their sense of belongingness to society increases. The scheme has the potential of reducing exploitative phenomena like child labour and gender discrimination. In particular, it holds the powerful prospect of bringing major changes in the lives of women. This Act has the potential to bring drastic change in the lives of rural women. It gives an opportunity to women to come out of their shell and which alone can lead to their empowerment.

MGNREGA also has a positive impact on education specially at the pre-primary and primary level. As all the adult members of the family work under MGNREGA, children of the family are sent to government schools. Government schools also provide mid day meal which makes the school the best place for the parents to keep their children. Subsequently, there is increase in the number of students enrolled in school.

MGNREGA provides an opportunity to the rural people to plan the work to be carried out and the implementation of the act themselves. The *gram sabha* recommends the work to be taken up under the MGNREGA and identifies the persons to work under the scheme. It also brings about transparency at the grass root level through social audits on implementation of the Act conducted by the *gram sabha*. The Act sets an example of democratic decentralization. The institution of *panchayati raj* will get strengthened through MGNREGA. It is the first act, which has given an excellent opportunity to the *panchayats* to prove their mettle. For the first time, *panchayats* have got the power to make schemes, implement them and money is no more a constraint.

Water and soil conservation works continue to be on high priority. Drought proofing and flood protection aim to provide resistance to climate shocks and natural disasters. Thus, MGNREGA can actually be seen to be moving towards food and livelihood security and long term sustainable development through ecological regeneration. In Rajasthan, majority of the work undertaken are related with water conservation and rural connectivity. Besides these, MGNREGA has been converged with various public works related to agriculture, water resources, land resources, environment and forest and rural connectivity under the related departments and institutes for sustainable development. Availability of untied funds for local area planning also encourages convergence for sustainable development. MGNREGA can bring about both economic and ecological sustainability.

Observations from Field Study

In twenty nine states of India, the same central policy is implemented with twenty eight variations. Interestingly this study is about intrastate variations. The state of Rajasthan has been a dry region where frequent drought and famines are reported. This leaves the agricultural farmers in distress. Rajasthan has also played a prime role in the enactment of MGNREGA with its people's movements. There are also positive reports from Rajasthan of other rural policies of government of India. The four districts of Rajasthan i.e. Dungarpur, Jhalawar, Sirohi and Udaipur were selected for the study since MGNREGA was implemented in the first phase in these districts. Further, these districts have been identified by the Planning Commission as backward districts of the country on the basis of three main parameters[1]. These districts have been identified with low wage, low agricultural productivity and high SC and ST population. Moreover, these districts have high out-migration because of recurrent droughts and low agricultural productivity.

The main parameters adopted in this study to assess the performance of the policy in the four districts are participation, awareness level, duration of getting job on demand, payment related issues, worksite facilities and overall impact.

On the basis of these parameters the districts have been graded in a scale of 1-4 in terms of their effectiveness in implementing the Act. The grading will be done on the basis of maximum number of grade points given to a district. The following Table II depicts the performance of the districts and their grading. According to the grading, Sirohi has been graded as1; Udaipur -2; Dungarpur- 3; and Jhalawar - 4. Sirohi has got maximum number of grade 1 points followed by Udaipur.

When we compare the parameters of implementing the policy, the policy has been best implemented at Sirohi. Sirohi is the best performer among the four districts with its maximum grade 1 points.

There are certain factors which have been identified for effective implementation of the Act in Sirohi. One of the major factors is that Sirohi is one of the poorest districts in Rajasthan with about 31 percent of the population living below the poverty line. It is also one of the districts close to Gujarat, where large scale migration takes place during drought. For the poor people living in rural areas the employment provided by MGNREGA is significant for their livelihood. The demand for work is also very high. Because of its demand-driven approach, implementing agencies are duty-bound to generate work for them.

Table 6.1: Grading of the Four Districts in Terms of Their Implementation of MGNREGA

No. of People Who Received JC within 10-15 days		**Grade**
Dungarpur*	10.0% (better condition)	2
Jhalawar*	10.0%(sad condition)	3
Sirohi	0	4
Udaipur	11.6%	1
No. of People Who Got Employment within 15-20 days		**Grade**
Dungarpur	8.3%	4
Jhalawar	16.6%	2
Sirohi	11.6%	3
Udaipur	18.3%	1
No. of People Who Worked for Maximum No. of Days(80-100 Days)		**Grade**
Dungarpur	38.3%	3
Jhalawar	21.6%	4
Sirohi	63.3%	1
Udaipur	58.3%	2
No. of People Who Received Maximum Wage Per Day(Rs.100 & above)		**Grade**
Dungarpur	23.3%	3
Jhalawar	33.3%	2
Sirohi	66.6%	1
Udaipur	6.6%	4
No. of People Who Received Payment within 15 days -1 month		**Grade**
Dungarpur	18.3%	3
Jhalawar	16.6%	4
Sirohi	41.6%	1
Udaipur	21.6%	2
No. of People Who Come Beyond 5 km		**Grade**
Dungarpur	5.0%	2
Jhalawar	15.0%	4
Sirohi	2.0%	1
Udaipur	6.6%	3

(Contd...)

No. of People Aware about Gram Sabha Held		Grade
Dungarpur	26.6%	3
Jhalawar	21.6%	4
Sirohi	45.0%	1
Udaipur	36.6%	2
No. of People Who Received Signed Receipt		**Grade**
Dungarpur	8.3%	2
Jhalawar	5.0%	3
Sirohi	11.6%	1
Udaipur	1.6%	4

*Since the percentage of people received JC within 15-20 days in Dungarpur and Jhalawar is same, grading has been given on the basis of the condition of the JC.

A 2Qs (quality and quantity) assessment of NREGS in Sirohi, by the CUTS Centre for Consumer Action, Research and Training (CUTS CART) in partnership with the World Bank has also revealed 97 per cent employment was provided by MGNREGA for the inhabitants in their own villages during the lean season. The scheme has helped bring down migration by 93 per cent and helped improve facilities in the villages by 94 per cent[2].

For a successful implementation of MGNREGA, the participation of beneficiaries is very important because employment is provided on the basis of self identification of beneficiaries. The participative nature of the beneficiaries can be credited to the implementation of previous government policies from which many of them have benefitted. Due to this, the people in Sirohi were proactive in their approach. Thereby, it puts an obligation on the government to provide work on demand.

NGOs like Jan Chetna Sansthan(JCS)[3] work in the villages of Sirohi to support the people to attain their rights through organized and collective effort. The major thrust of JCS is to make people aware of their rights and build their capacities through social education, training and information dissemination to take collective action to resolve their issues. This NGO has been working actively in Sirohi to sensitise the rural poor. It has been intervening in the policy making and implementation of various government policies. Policy intervention programme is one of the main objectives of the JCS. The presence of such Civil Society Organisations have led to the active participation of people and effective implementation of government policies.

The earlier experiences of government policies have made the people of Sirohi more vocal about their rights. Moreover, the ST population in this area mainly comprises of *adivasis* (tribals). This group of people prefer to work for their livelihood within their community. This may be one of the factors that Sirohi has provided maximum days of work to most of the beneficiaries. There was visible distinction between the *adivasis* and other workers at the worksite.

The highest wage to the beneficiaries was also paid in Sirohi. They unanimously raise their concerns about increasing the wage rate and other entitlements of which they are aware. This has resulted in a better wage rate in the area. The women workforce also demands that payment should be made at par with men. Therefore, there is no scope for discrimination in the payment of wages.

It was also found that block level officers were sincere in their effort in implementing the policy. They were well aware of the guidelines of implementing MGNREGA issued by the MoRD. They constantly monitor and supervise the implementation of the programme. An innovative way of addressing the grievances of the beneficiaries was seen. Since many of the beneficiaries share the same space with *panchayat* functionaries, they do not complain or talk about their grievances. They do not want to spoil their cordial relationship with the PRI members. The B.D.O. at Abu Road has kept a box (shown in Picture 5.1) for the beneficiaries to drop their complaints in the box. The B.D.O checks the box in a routine manner and tries to address their problems. He also added that he visits the worksites regularly to monitor the works and verification of JC is done at the ground level by the *panchayat.* Similarly, the B.D.O in Pindwara has given his mobile number to the beneficiaries so that they can directly call him in case their grievances are not addressed. He also said that the administration is over burdened. Eighty percent of the administration is involved in the implementation of MGNREGA. Out of all the government programmes, MGNREGA is implemented on a priority basis.

It is also the participative nature of the beneficiaries which have made the implementing agencies and government officials to work promptly.

We cannot deny the fact that there are drawbacks in the implementation of the policy in Sirohi. Like, many of the beneficiaries were working without a JC. JC is meant for identifying the households and a legal document to maintain transparency. Yet employment was provided without a JC. There was also delay in providing employment on demand. There are cases where people from good economic conditions are working under MGNREGA because the Act guarantees employment to any rural household who demand for work. With the limited generation of work, the benefit of the rural poor is may drift away.

Picture 6.1: Complaint Box at B.D.O. in Abu Road, Sirohi

Next to Sirohi, it is Udaipur where the policy is implemented in a proper manner. In Udaipur, JC was provided on time to majority of the population. JC is a legal document which ensures that there is accountability and transparency. Although the demand for work in Udaipur was less, work was provided on time. There is a pressure on the implementing agencies to adhere to the guidelines of the Act. However, the active participation of beneficiaries in Udaipur was lacking. The awareness level among the beneficiaries was also low. But, the policy has brought some social changes in the lives of the deprived old people and women in the area. The main factor which is responsible for the effective implementation of the policy in Udaipur is the strong bureaucratic will. The active supervision and monitoring by the officials of the execution of the policy at the ground level has led to efficiency in the policy. But unlike, Sirohi the people were not vocal and actively participating.

The district of Dungarpur has been declared one of the best implemented districts by the Ministry of Rural Development. Studies have also shown that the implementation in MGNREGA in Dungarpur has been positive[4, 5]. But my study carried out in the two *gram panchayats* did not show a very promising picture. The prominent factor for the poor performance in Dungarpur is lack of coordination among the stakeholders. The vertical as well horizontal coordination among the implementing agencies was poor. There was a communication gap among the panchayat functionaries as well as with the government officials. So, the Act is implemented in a haphazard manner. For an effective implementation of the policy, a well coordinated strategy is needed which was lacking in Dungarpur. The block level officers were not available for interview during my field study so, it will be difficult to comment much. However, interaction with beneficiaries, villagers and *panchayat* members, revealed that there is lack of monitoring and supervision by higher authorities. That is why there are delays in providing employment, wages and other benefits to the workers.

Among the four districts, the policy is worst implemented in Jhalawar. There was low participation of the beneficiaries due to low awareness level. Since the beneficiaries were mostly illiterate, the implementing agencies blatantly violate the Act. There were discrepancies in the payment of wages to the workers. The workers were found to be unhappy about the transparency and accountability factor in the implementation of the Act. Yet, there was no effective grievance redress mechanism in place to address the grievances of the workers. The Panchayat functionaries were not actively involved in the implementation of the policy and were found to be unaware about the ground realities in their area. Similarly, the officials complained of over burdened administrative work so they are unable to monitor the work. Lack of awareness among the beneficiaries, inactive *panchayat* members, dishonest mate at the worksite and lethargic bureaucrats are some of the factors which emerged for poor implementation of the policy in Jhalawar.

From the above discussion, it is clear that there are intrastate variations in Rajasthan in the implementation of MGNREGA.

Recommendations

There are some policy recommendations on the basis of the findings of the study. MGNREGA is a self targeted programme for benefits to the poor. There is no specific criterion for identifying the poor and needy households under MGNREGA. The demand-driven approach of the programme relies on the beneficiaries to select themselves. This ensures that the targeted population is benefitted. There is lack of work to gratify the demand for jobs under the scheme. It has been found that there are non-poor households who obstruct the employment of poor households when there is inadequate work. This phenomenon has been described as "Capture" which means the benefits of the poor is blocked by the non-poor. Many studies have also reported that the benefits of the pro-poor policies are often captured by the non-poor. This has been cited as one of the major challenges in the effective implementation of policies like MGNREGA.[6]

Employment should be given on a priority basis to those households who are in need of income for their livelihood. The criteria of providing employment to households need to be redefined. A household with large members are unable to get the benefit of the Act. The number of days of providing employment should be increased on the basis of the size of the household.

It is worth mentioning that most of the beneficiaries are illiterate, which is one of the primary reasons behind their unawareness of the statutory norms. The participation of beneficiaries in the implementation process of a policy is needed for successful implementation of MGNREGA. In this regard, we can say that educating MGNREGA workers can facilitate their ability to understand the scheme. The National Literacy Mission programme of the Government of India for spreading adult education can be supportive in this effort. It can help the workers become acquainted with their rights and benefits more clearly and voice their demands. This will also increase the accountability factor among the higher implementing agencies. MGNREGA can be linked with major policies of the Government of India being implemented in the rural areas. This can enhance effective implementation of other policies of the government. Government should encourage the formation of SHG (Self Help Groups) which shall proliferate the information about the act and its nuances. Civil Society Organisations can also play a prominent role in raising the awareness among the beneficiaries.

The Act can play a significant role in the enrolment of rural children to schools. Since proper worksite facilities are not provided at the worksites and majority of workers are women, they send their children to nearby government schools. In government schools, they not only get educated but also get Mid Day Meals[7] which help the women of the household to work. This will ensure that the children get enrolled in school. The young children (3–5 years) can also be sent to *anganwadi* centres' created under the Integrated Child Development Services (ICDS). It will also help the children in improving their health and nurture them for schooling.

Another important issue which arises is the sustainability of the programme. We have seen that the demand for work is not fulfilled because of paucity of work. There is need to bring changes so that more work can be accommodated in the scheme. If timely employment is not generated timely, the positive socio-economic changes related with the scheme may go to waste. Integrated approaches in the implementation of government policies can fill in the gaps to a certain extent. The capacity of the *panchayat* functionaries needs to be developed by providing them rigorous training from time to time with practical experiences. This will help them to plan and create more useful work for the village and provide timely work to the beneficiaries. This will in turn help in developing rural asset and increase rural economy. There shall be increase in exchange of ideas within various *panchayat* members and governing officials through common meetings so that the story of one success can be heard by all and emulated too.

It has been seen that often the *panchayats* provide work on the basis of their relationship with the beneficiaries. The politicization of providing work under the scheme has to be curtailed. The higher implementing agency needs to be more responsive for ensuring an effective implementation of the Act.

There is a necessity to strengthen the grievance redressal mechanisms. There is also a need to encourage the beneficiaries to come up with their grievances. The fear psychosis that they will not get work if they complain needs to be broken. The ability of the poor to voice their rights needs to be improved which can be a positive step towards the realization of poverty eradication. They should be made aware of the Right to Information act. It can be an effective tool realising their rights.

The Act will be very effective in addressing the acute problem of poverty in India. A strong monitoring teams needs to be developed to keep vigil on the implementation of the policy. The need of the hour is to take this Act seriously and check the loopholes of the Act. The responsibility of checking the problems in the policy should not only rest with the government. Civil society, local communities and *Panchayati Raj* Institutions should involve actively in its planning and implementation. This will help in checking the implementation problems and also prevent wastage of public money invested in the scheme.

The implementation of MGNREGA has been uneven across the country. In some areas, the Act has begun to demonstrate its potential. However, in most parts of the country the basic prerequisite of a meaningful legal entitlement for the rural citizen is still to be put in place. The first priority of the government must be to ensure that the basic framework is in place across the country, and that citizens in all parts of rural India can exercise their right to work on demand, minimum wages, timely payments, etc. Thus, MGNREGA needs to be nurtured to bring about socio-economic changes.

As the milieu of the rural poor improves due to this act some positive effects on the rural environment can be expected. Children in rural areas can be expected to acquire better education as their parent's frequency of movement reduces and they have more money in their hands. The village environment also improves because most of these works are directed towards projects to counter problems like drought, soil erosion, deforestation, etc.

Rajasthan being a drought prone area where there is no livelihood security, the Act will provide social security to the rural poor. This Act can bring some respite to the rural poor and the villages are an example of how the Act can bring changes in the lives of the rural poor. The significance of the Act lies in the fact that the Act has had a positive impact on the people even if there are still certain shortcomings in its implementation.

MGNREGA should be continued with more rigorous implementation. In the near future it is to be expected that only such radical acts will have a lasting impact on the economy, society and environment of India which aim at inclusive growth through a right based approach to development. This is a kind of growth that India can sustain for generations ahead.

Bibliography

1. Abhay (2006) "Status of National Rural Employment Guarantee Scheme in Raichur, Karnataka"; Satyagraha for NREGs on 14-15 August 2007 at Raichur, Karnataka
2. Acharya, Shankar (2004a) "Bad Ideas Are Winning"; Business Standard, 28 December.
3. ___ (2004b) "Guaranteeing Jobs or a Fiscal Crisis?" Business Standard, 30 November.
4. Acharya, Shankar (2005) "Populism Rides Again"; Business Standard, 27 December.
5. Ahuja, Ram (2005) "Research Methods";Rawat Publications,Jaipur.
6. Aiyar, Swaminathan S. Anklesaria (2004) "Poverty Reduction by Helicopter"; Times of India, 19 December.
7. Aiyar, Y. and S. Samji (2006) "Improving the Effectiveness of National Rural Employment Guarantee Act"; Economic and Political Weekly, 28 January, 41 (4): 320-6.
8. ___ (2009) "Transparency and Accountability in NREGA: A Case Study of Andhra Pradesh"; Working Paper, Accountability Initiative, Centre for Policy Research, New Delhi.
9. Ambasta, P., P.S Vijay Shankar and M. Shah (2008) "Two Years of NREGA: The Road Ahead"; Economic and Political Weekly, 23 February, 43 (8): 41-50.
10. Anderson, James E (1975) "Public Policy Making"; Praeger, New York
11. Asha Parivar (2006) "Findings of Social Audit of NREGS in Bharawan and Sandila Blocks of Hardoi District in U.P. during 25th November-2nd December".
12. Bagchee, Aruna (2005) "Political and Administrative Realities of the EGS"; Economic and Political Weekly, 15 October, 40 (43): 4531-7.

13. Bailey, L. (1982) "Methods of Social Research."; The Free Press, New York.

14. Balagopal, K. (2006) "Chhattisgarh: Physiognomy of Violence"; Economic and Political Weekly, 3 June, 41 (22): 2183-6.

15. Benbabbaali, Dalel (2009) "Implementation of the National Rural Employment Guarantee Act in a Tribal State: Meghalaya", mimeo.

16. Bandyopadhyay, D (1988) "Direct Intervention Programmes for Poverty Alleviation: An Appraisal"; Economic and Political Weekly, 25 June: A77-A88.

17. Banerjee, A and P. Bardhan (2004) "Food for Thought"; Hindustan Times, 15 December.

18. Banerjee, K. and P. Saha (2010) "The NREGA, the Maoists and the Development Woes of Indian State"; Economic and Political Weekly, 10 July, 45 (28): 42-8.

19. Bardach, Eugene (1974) "The Implementation Game: What Happens After a Bill

20. Becomes Law"; MIT Press, Cambridge, MA.

21. Barrett, Susan and Colin Fudge (1981)" Examining the policy action relationship" in Susan Barrett and Colin Fudge (eds.) *Policy and Action*; Methuen, London.

22. Barret, B.C., S. Holden, and D.C. Clay (2002) "Can Food-for-Work Programme Reduce Vulnerability?" Discussion Paper 2002/24; World Institute for Development Economics Research, Helsinki.

23. Berman, P. (1978) "The Study of Macro and Micro Implementation"; Public Policy; 26(2):157-84

24. Besley, T. and S. Coate (1992) "Workfare vs Welfare: Incentive Arguments for Work Requirements in Poverty Alleviation Programmmes"; American Economic Review, 82 (1): 249-61.

25. Bhaduri, Amit (2005) "Development with Dignity: A Case for Full Employment"; National Book Trust, New Delhi.

26. Bhalla, Sheila (2005) "India's Rural Economy: Issues and Evidence"; Institute of Human Development, New Delhi.

27. Bhalla, Surjit S. (2004a) "Corruption with a Human Face"; Business Standard, 11 December.

28. ___ Bhalla, Surjit S. (2004b) "Ten Lies and an Act: I"; Business Standard, 25 December.

29. Bharagava, Rajeev (2006) "Indian Democracy and Well-Being: Employment as a Right"; Public Culture, 18 (3): 445-51.

30. Bhardwaj, K. K. "Hemu-Napoleon of Medieval India", Mittal Publications, New Delhi, p.25

31. Bhatia, Bela (2008) "Salwa Judum: Internal War as Counter-Insurgency", mimeo, National Institute of Rural Development; also partly reprinted in Bhatia, B. (2008) Aspects of the Naxalite Movement in India, report to the Indian Council of Social Science Research.

32. Bhatia, Bela and Jean Drèze (2006) "Employment Guarantee in Jharkhand: Ground Realitites"; Economic and Political Weekly, 22 July, 49 (23): 3198-202.

33. Bhatia, Kartika (2009) "NREGA: A Guarantee against Migration?" mimeo, G.B. Pant Social Science Institute, Allahabad.

34. Bhatty, Kiran (2006) "Employment Guarantee and Child Rights"; Economic and Political Weekly, 20 May, 41 (20): 1965-7.

35. Bhatty, Kiran (2006) "Social Equality and Development: Himachal Pradesh and Its Wider Significance"; PhD thesis submitted to the London School of Economics.

36. Birkland, Thomas A (2005) "An Introduction to the Policy Process: Theories, Concepts and Models of Public Policy Making", (2nd ed) Armonk, M.E. Sharpe, New York

37. Bisht, Arvind Singh (2006) "Rural Employment: No Guarantee Yet"; Times of India, 19 February.

38. Breman, Jan (1996) "Footloose Labour: Working in India's Informal Economy"; Contemporary South Asia Series. Cambridge University Press, Cambridge.

39. ___ (2003) "The Labouring Poor in India: Patterns of Exploitation: Subordination and Exclusion";Oxford University Press, New Delhi.

40. Brewer, G. D. and deLeon, P. (1983) "The Foundations of Policy Analysis", Brooks/Cole, Monterey, CA.

41. Business standard (2010) "Rajasthan Agrees to NREGA Workers' Demand"; Business Standard, November 18, 2010, New Delhi.

42. Centre for Budget and Governance Accountability (2006) "Draft Report on Implementation of NREGA in Andhra Pradesh, Chhattisgarh, Jharkhand and Madhya Pradesh", Report. Centre for Budget and Governance Accountability, New Delhi.

43. Centre for Planning, Monitoring and Evaluation (2008) "Evaluation of Implementation of NREGS in Orissa", Social Audit Report; National Institute for Rural Development, Hyderabad.

44. Centre for Science and Environment (CSE) (2008) "NREGA: Opportunities and Challenges" CSE, New Delhi.

45. Centre for Science and Environment (CSE) (2008) "An Ecological Act: A Backgrounder to the National Employment Guarantee Scheme" CSE, New Delhi. Available at: http://www.world-governance.org/IMG/pdf_572__NREGA_Briefing_CSE.pdf.

46. Chakraborty Pinaki (2007a) "Implementation of Employment Guarantee: A Preliminary Appraisal"; Economic and Political Weekly, February 17,2007.pp.548-551.

47. ___ (2007b) "Implementation of the National Rural Employment Guarantee Act in India: Spatial Dimensions and Fiscal Implementation"; Working Paper No. 55, NIPFPF and the Levy Economics Institute, July 2007.

48. Chakraborty, P., C.B. Rao, D.K. Srivastava, and S.K. Sanyal (2007) "Rural Poverty in Madhya Pradesh: Looking Beyond Conventional Measures"; Economic and Political Weekly, 3 February, 42 (5): 381-8.

49. Chari, Anurekha (2006) "Guaranteed Employment and Gender Construction: Women's Mobilisation in Maharashtra"; Economic and Political Weekly, 16 December, 41 (50): 5141-8.

50. Chary, Venkat R. (2005) "REGS: Grossly Miscalculated?" Hindu Business Line, 9 September.

51. Chathukulam, J. and K.Gireesan (2007) "Impact Assessment of NREGS in Kerala:Evaluation of Systems and Processes";mimeo, Centre for Rural Management, Kerala.

52. Chaupal, Sansthan (2010) "Study of Implementation of MGNREGA in Chattishgarh"; mimeo, Chaupal Gramin Vikas Prashikshan Evam Shodh Sansthan, Ambikapur.

53. Chaurasia, Radhey Shyam (2002) "History of Ancient India: Earliest Times to 1000 A. D"; Atlantic Publishers & Distributors, New Delhi.

54. Chen, Martha (1989) "Women's Work in Indian Agriculture by Agro-Ecologic Zones:Meeting Needs of Landless and Land-Poor Women"; Economic and Political Weekly, 28 October, 24 (43) : WS 79-89.

55. Cherian, Thomas (2005) "Adding Jobs But at What Cost?" International Herald Tribune, 14 September.

56. Chikermance, Gautam(2008) "It is not Worth CAG's While to Look at Rs.100 Telephone Bills or Rs.200 Staff Car Bills"; Indian Express, 13 February.

57. Clay, E. J. and Schaffer, B. B (1986) "Room for Manoeuvre: An Explanation of Public Policy in Agriculture and Rural Development"; Heinemann, London.

58. CUTS Centre for Consumer Action, Research & Training (2008) "Assessing 2Qs (Quality & Quantity) Outputs of the 'National Rural Employment Guarantee Scheme' (NREGS), as per provisions of NREGA (2005) in Sirohi District of Rajasthan, India"; CUTS Centre for Consumer Action, Research & Training, In partnership with the World Bank, Jaipur

59. Dale, Reider (1998) "Evaluation Frameworks for Development Programmes and Projects"; Sage Publication, London

60. Daneke, Gregory A. and Alan Walter Steiss(1978) "Planning and Policy Analysis for Public Administrators" in John W. Sutherland (ed.) *Management Handbook for Public Administrators;* Van Nostrand and Reinhold Company, New York.

61. De, Prabir Kumar (2011) "Public Policy and System"; Pearson, New Delhi.

62. Peter de Leon (1999) "The Missing Link Revisited: Contemporary Implementation Research"; Policy Studies Review 16: 311–339.

63. Peter de Leon and Linda de Leon (2002) "What Ever Happened to Policy Implementation? An Alternative Approach"; Journal of Public Administration Research and Theory 12: 467–492.

64. de Leon, Peter and Danielle M. Vogenbeck(2007a) "Back to Square One:The History and Promise of the Policy Sciences" in Jack Rabin, et.al(ed.) *Handbook of Public Policy Administration,* CRC Press, Taylor and Francis Group, Florida pg.504

65. ___ de Leon,Peter and Danielle M. Vogenbeck(2007b) "The Policy Sciences at the Crossroads" in Frank Fischer, et.al (ed.), *Handbook of Public Policy Analysis Theory,Politics and Methods,*CRC Press,Taylor and Francis Group, Florida pg4-5

66. Denzin, N.K. (1970) "The Research Act in Sociology";Aldine, Chicago.

67. Derthick, Martha (1972) "New Towns In-Town: Why a Federal Program Failed"; The Urban Institute, Washington, DC

68. Dey,Nikhil, Jean Drèze and Reetika Khera(2006) "Employment Guarantee Act:A Primer"; National Book Trust, New Delhi.

69. Dey, Nikhil and Aruna Roy (2009) "Dalits,Poor and the NREGA"; The Hindu, 27 August.

70. Jean Drèze, (2004a) "Employment as Social Responsibility"; The Hindu,21 November

71. ___ (2004b) "Why Should Anyone be Afraid of the Employment Guarantee Act?"; Financial Express,18 December

72. ___ (2004c) "Unemployment Guarantee Bill";The Hindu,31 December

73. ___ (2005a) "Employment Guarantee and its Discontents"; The Times of India,12 August

74. ___ (2005b) "Totally Off Target: Employment Guarantee and Its Discontents";The Times of India,12 August

75. ___ (2005c) "Time to Clean Up: Employment Guarantee and Its Discontents";The Times of India,13 August

76. ___ (2006) "National Employment Guarantee Act Inaction";The Hindu, 12 September

77. ___ (2007a) "Dismantaling the Contractor Raj";The Hindu, November

78. ___ (2007b) "India's Employment Guarantee Act: Reclaiming Policy Space"; in A. Deshpande (ed.)*Globalization and Development*, Oxford University Press, New Delhi

79. ___ (2008a) "Employment Guarantee: Beyond Propaganda"; The Hindu,11 January

80. ___ (2008b) "Lok Adalat or Joke Adalat"; The Hindu,22 February

81. ___ (2008c) "Ship Without Rudder";The Hindu,19 July

82. ___ (2009) "Act Fair, Give Rural Workers Their Due"; The Times of India,12 July

83. ___ (2011) "Employment Guarantee and the Right to Work" in Reetika Khera (ed.) *The Battle for Employment Guarantee*; Oxford University Press, New Delhi.

84. Drèze, Jean and Siddhartha Lal (2007) "Employment Guarantee: Unfinished Agenda";The Hindu,13 July

85. Drèze, Jean and Chris Oldiges (2007) "Commendable Act"; Frontline,27 July

86. Drèze, Jean and Sowmya Kidambi (2007) "Long Road to Employment Guarantee";The Hindu, 2 August

87. Drèze, Jean and Reetika Khera (2008) "From Accounts to Accountability"; The Hindu, 6 December

88. ___ (2009a) "Banned But Still There"; Frontline,16 January

89. ___ (2009b) "The Battle for Employment Guarantee"; Frontline,16 January
90. Drèze, Jean, Reetika Khera and Siddhartha(2008) "Corruption in NREGA: Myths and Realities"; The Hindu,22 January
91. Drèze, Jean and Siddhartha(2009) "Flaws System";Frontline,16 January
92. Drèze, Jean and Chris Oldiges (2009) "Work in Progress"; Frontline,14th February
93. Dror, Yehezkel (1968) "Public Policy Making Re-examined";Chandler Publishing Company, USA.
94. ___ (1971) "Design for Policy Sciences" American Elsevier, New York.
95. Dunn, Edgar S. (1971) "Economic and Social Development: A Process of Social Learning"; The John Hopkins University Press, Baltimore.
96. Dutta, Puja, Rinku Murgai, Martin Ravallion and Dominique Van de Walle (2012) "Does India's Employment Guarantee Scheme Guarantee Employment?"; Economic and Political Weekly,, 2012 Vol. XLVII No. 16, April.pp.55-64
97. Dye, Thomas (2004) "Understanding Public Policy"; (10th ed.) Pearson, New Delhi.
98. Easton, David (1968) "A framework for Political Analysis", Englewood Cliffs: Prentice-Hall.
99. Friedrich, Carl J.(1963) "Man and His Government";McGraw Hill, New York.
100. Friend, J.K., J.M. Power and C.J.L.Yewlett (1974) "Public Planning: The Inter- Corporate Dimension"; Tavistock, London.
101. Frohock, Fred M.(1979) "Public Policy: Scope and Logic";Prentice Hall,Englewood Cliffs.
102. Froman, Lewis A. (1967) Jr., "An Analysis of Public Policies in Cities," Journal of Politics, XXIX February,pg.94-108.
103. Gabrielian, Vatche (1999) "Qualitative Research Method: An Overview" in Gerald J.Miller and Marcia L. Whicker (ed.) *Handbook of Research Method in Public Administration;* Marcel Dekker, New York
104. Ghosh, Jayati (2006) "The 'Right to Work' and Recent Legislation in India"; Social Scientist, Vol.34.No.1/2 (Jan-Feb,2006), pp.88-102.

105. Goggin,Malcolm Ann O'M. Bowman, James Lester, and Laurence O'Toole Jr. (1990) "Implementation Theory and Practice: Towards a Third Generation"; Foresman Scott / Brown Little Glenview, Illinios.

106. Lester, James and Malcolm Goggin (1998) "Back to the Future: The Rediscovery of Implementation Studies"; Policy Currents, September: 1–7.

107. Goodin, Robert E., Martin Rein and Michael Moran (2006) "The public and its Policies" in Robert E. Goodin et.al (ed.) *The Oxford Handbook of Public Policy*; Oxford University Press, New York.

108. Goswami, Anupam (2008): "Jobs for the Poor", Business India, Feb.10, 2008.

109. Government of India (1973) "Report of the Committee on Unemployment (Bhagwati Committee)"; Government of India, New Delhi.

110. ___ (1975) "Report on Evaluation Study of Small Farmers,Marginal Farmers and Agricultural Labourers Project, 1974-75;Chapter 6; Planning Commission, Government of India, New Delhi.

111. ___ (1977) "Report of the Review Committee on Pilot Intensive Rural Employment Project (PIREP), Ministry of Irrigation and Agriculture, Government of India, New Delhi.

112. ___ (1979) "Study of Crash Scheme for Rural Employment"; Programme Evaluation Organization(PEO),Study No.104, Planning Commission, Government of India, New Delhi.

113. ___ (1980) "Evaluation of Food for Work Programme"; Programme Evaluation Organization(PEO),Study No.114, Planning Commission, Government of India, New Delhi.

114. ___ (2000a) "Evaluation of Study on Employment Assurance Scheme"; Programme Evaluation Organization(PEO), Planning Commission, Government of India, New Delhi

115. ___ (2000b) "Ninth Five Year Plan, 2002-07"; Vol.II; Planning Commission, Government of India, New Delhi.

116. ___ (2002) "Tenth Five Year Plan, 2002-07"; Vol.III; Planning Commission, Government of India, New Delhi.

117. ___ (2003) "Report of the Task Force on: Identification of Districts for Wage and Self Employment Programmes"; Planning Commission, Government of India.

118. ___ (2005) "The Gazette of India"; Extraordinary, Part II-Section 1,No.48;Ministry of Law and Justice, Government of India, New Delhi

119. ___ (2006a) "61st Round Report of National Sample Survey Organisation", July 2004-June 2005, Ministry of Statistics and Programme Implementation, Government of India, New Delhi.

120. ___ (2006b) "Unlocking Human Capital: Entitlements and Governance- A Case Study"; Second Administrative Commission Report.

121. (Also available on http://arc.gov.in)

122. ___ (2007a) "Eleventh Five Year Plan,Vol.I,II & III"; Planning Commission, Government of India.

123. ___ (2007b) "Performance Audit of Implementation of National Rural Employment Guarantee Act, 2005 (NREGA) draft report"; Comptroller and Auditor General, New Delhi.

124. ___ (2010) "Mahatma Gandhi National Rural Employment Guarantee Act, 2005(MGNREGA), Report to the People";Ministry of Rural Development, New Delhi. (Also available at www.nrega.nic.in)

125. ___ (2011a) "Census of India, Office of the Registrar General and Census Commissioner"; Government of India.

126. ___ (2011b) "Economic Survey of India 2010-11"; Ministry of Finance, Government of India, New Delhi.

127. Government of Rajasthan and Institute of Development Studies(2008) " Human Development Report Rajasthan: An Update-2008"; A Study Conducted by the Institute of Development Studies, Jaipur for the Government of Rajasthan and Planning Commission of India in GoI and UNDP assisted project "Strengthening State Plans for Human Development".

128. ___ (2009a) "Dungarpur District Human Development Report,2009"; A Study Conducted by the Institute of Development Studies, Jaipur for the Government of Rajasthan and Planning Commission of India.

129. ___ (2009b) "Jhalawar District Human Development Report,2009"; A Study Conducted by the Institute of Development Studies, Jaipur for the Government of Rajasthan and Planning Commission of India.

130. Government of Rajasthan (2012) "Economic Review 2011-12";Planning Department, Directorate of Economics and Statistics, Rajasthan.

131. Gupta, R.K. and S.R. Bakshi(2008) "Studies in Indian History, Rajasthan Through the Ages: Heritage of Rajputs (Vol.1)";Sarup and Sons, New Delhi

132. Hanekom, S.X. & Thornhill, C. (1993) "Public Administration in Contemporary Society: A South African Perspective"; Revised edition. Southern, Pretoria.

133. Hargrove, Erwin C. (1975) "The Missing Link: The Study of the Implementation of Social Policy"; Urban Institute, Washington, DC.

134. Harris, P. (1990) "Foundation of Public Administration: A Comparative Approach" University Press, Hong Kong.

135. Hirway, Indira, M.R. Saluja and Bhupesh Yadav (2010) "Employment Guarantee Programme and the Pro-Poor Growth: The Study of a Village in Gujarat"; Academic Foundation, New Delhi.

136. Hogwood, B.W. and L.A.Gunn(1984) "Policy Analysis for the Real World"; Oxford University Press, London.

137. Howlett, Michael and M. Ramesh (2003), "Studying Public Policy: Policy Cycles and Policy Subsystems", Oxford: Oxford University Press.

138. Institute of Applied Manpower Research (2007) "All India Report on Evaluation of NREGA: A Survey of Twenty Districts", Programme Evaluation Organisation (PEO), Planning Commission, Government of India.

139. Institute of Development Studies (IDS) (2008) "Evaluation of NREGA in Rajasthan', Report submitted to Ministry of Rural Development/UNDP, Jaipur: IDS, 2008.

140. Jaswal, Anshuman and Paulomee Mistry(2007) "Will NREGA Ensure Security Against Hunger?"; Disha. Available at: http://www.disha-india.org/Diwaspercent20Ugepercent20Nepercent20Dadipercent20Male.pdf

141. Jha,Raghbendra, Sambit Bhattacharyya, Raghav Gaiha and Shylashri Shankar (2009) "'Capture' of anti-poverty programs: An analysis of the Nation Rural Employment Guarantee Program in India"; Journal of Asian Economics"; Vol.20, pg.456-464.

142. Jones, C. O. (1977) "An Introduction to the Study of Public Policy, 2nd ed., Duxbury Press, North Scituate, MA

143. Juma, C. and Clark, N. (1995) "Policy research in sub-Saharan Africa: An Emploration"; Public Administration and Development, Vol. 15, pp121–137.

144. Kedia, Sapna (2008) "NREGA Summer Survey-Dungarpur Initial Observations"; Project Report,G.B.Pant Social Science Institute,Allahbad

145. Khera, Reetika and Nandini Nayak(2009) "Women Workers and Perceptions of the National Rural Guarantee Act", Economic and Political Weekly, Vol. XLIV No.43,October.

146. Kholi, Atul (1987) "The State and Poverty in India: The Politics of Reform"; Cambridge University Press, Cambridge.

147. Knoepfel, Peter, Corinne Larrue, Frederic Varone and Michael Hill (2007) "Public Policy Analysis"; The Policy Press, Great Britain,pp. 227-28

148. Krutilla, J.V. (1961) "Welfare Aspects of Benefit-Cost Analysis" Journal of Political Economy, 69, 226.

149. Lasswell, H. (1951) "The Policy Orientation" in D.Lerner and H.D.Lasswell(ed.) *The Policy Sciences*; Stanford University Press, Palo Alto, California.

150. __ (1971) "A Pre-View of Policy Sciences", American Elsevier. Also available at: http://www.policysciences.org/classicworks.cfm)

151. Lindblom, Charles E. and Edward J Woodhouse (1993) "The Policy Making Process" (3rd ed.) Prentice Hall, Englewood Cliffs, New Jersey.

152. Lowi, Theodre J(1972) "Four Systems of Policy, Politics, and Choice"; Public Administration Review, XXXIII (July-August 1972), 298-310.

153. Lipsky, Michael (1971) "Street Level Bureaucracy and The Analysis of Urban Reform"; Urban Affairs Quarterly. 6: 391–409.

154. Majone, Giandomenico and Aaron Wildavsky (1978) "Implementation as Evolution" in H. Freeman (ed.) *Policy Studies ReviewAnnual*; Sage, Beverly Hills. pp. 103–117

155. Majumdar, R.C.(19520 "Ancient India";Banarsidass Publishers Private Limited, Varanasi.

156. Manheim, Henry L. (1977) "Sociological Research: Philosophy & Methods"; The Dorsey Press,Illinois.

157. Marini, Frank (2000) "Public Administration" in M.Shafritz (ed) *Defining Public Administration: Selections from the International*

Encyclopaedia of Public Policy and Administration; Westview Press, USA

158. Marshall, Dimock E (1937) "The Study of Administration"; American Political Science Review, Feb 1937

159. Mathur, Navdeep and Kuldeep Mathur (2006) "Policy Analysis in India:Research Bases and Discursive Practices" in Frank Fischer, Gerald J.Miller and Marn S.Sidney (ed.) *Handbook of Public Policy Analysis:Theory Politics and Methods*; CRC Press, Florida, USA.

160. Mazmanian, D.A. and P.A. Sabatier (1983) "Implementation and Public Policy"; Glenview, Ill.: Scott, Foresman.

161. May, J. and A. Wildavsky (1978) "The Policy Cycle", Sage Publications, Beverly Hills, CA.

162. Mehrotra, Santosh (2008) "NREG Two Years On: Where Do We Go From Here?" Economic and Political Weekly; Vol.XLIII, No.31,August 02,2008.

163. Miller, John D.Bruce (1965) "The Nature of Politics"; Penguin Publishing, London.

164. Murphy, Jerome (1973) "The Education Bureaucracies Implement Novel Policy: The Politics of Title I of ESSA"; in Allan Sindler (ed.) *Policy and Polictics in America*; Little, Brown: Boston.

165. Nakamura, Robert and Frank Smallwood(1980) "The Politics of Policy Implementation"; St.Martin's Press, New York

166. National Federation of Indian Women (NIFW) (2008) "A Study on Socio-Economic Empowerment of Women under NREGA"; Ministry of Rural Development, Government of India.

167. Oslen, Wendy (2004) "Triangulation in Social Research: Qualitative and Quantitative Methods Can Really Be Mixed" in M. Holborn (ed.) *Development in Sociology;* Causeway Press, Oranskisk

168. Poister, Theodore H. (1978) "Public Program Analysis: Applied Research Methods"; University Park Press, Baltimore.

169. Pressman, Jeffrey, and Aaron Wildavsky (1973) "Implementation: How Great Expectations in Washington Are Dashed in Oakland" University of California Press, Berkeley.

170. Quade, Edward (1975) "Analysis for Public Decisions", Elsevier, New York.

171. Right to Food (2007) "Employment Guarantee Act: A Primer"; Right to Food Campaign Secretariat, New Delhi.

172. Roger W.Cobb and Charles D.Elder (1983) "Participation in

American Politics: The dynamics of Agenda Building"; (2nd ed.) John Hopkins University Press, Baltimore.

173. Rossi, P.H. and H. Freeman (1993) "Evaluation: A Systematic Approach" (2nd eds.) Sage, California.

174. Rural Technology & Business Incubator (2009) "Evaluation of NREGA in Tamil Nadu"; Indian Institute of Technology, Madras.

175. Sabatier, P.A. and D. Mazmanian (1979) "The Conditions of Effective Implementation: A Guide To Accomplishing Objectives"; Policy Analysis, 484-5.

176. Samarthan-Centre for Development Support (2006) "Status of NREGA Implementation: Grassroots Learning and Ways Forward"; 1st Monitoring Report. Available at: http://www.empowerpoor.org/downloads/Status%20of%20NREGA%20in%20PACS%20states.pdf. Accessed on 20.5.2012

177. Sapru, R.K. (2004) "Public Policy: Formulation, Implementation and Evaluation"; Sterling Publication, New Delhi

178. Sapru, R.K. (2011) "Public Policy: Art and Craft of Policy Analysis"; PHI Learning Pvt. Ltd, New Delhi

179. Schattschneider, E.E. (1961) "The Semi Sovereign People"; Holt, Rinehart and Winston, New York.

180. Scott, James C (1969) "Corruption, Machine Politics, and Political Change"; American Political Science Review; Vol.63, No. 4; pp 1142-1158.

181. Shah, Mihir (2007) "Employment Guarantee, Civil Society and Indian Democracy"; Economic and Political Weekly, Vol.XLII No.45-46,November 10,2007.

182. Simon, Herbert A.(1957) "Administrative Behaviour";Free Press, New York.

183. ___ (1964) "On the Concept of Organisational Goal"; Administrative Science Quarterly, Vol.9; No.1, June.

184. Smith, M. (1988) "Strategies and Social Research"; Prentice Hall, Englewood Cliffs.

185. Smith, Thomas B (1973) "The Policy Implementation Process"; Policy Sciences; Vol.4, No.2; pp 197-209.

186. Smith, Kevin B. and Christopher W.Larimer(2009) " The Public Policy Theory Primer", Westview Press, Central Avenue, Boulder, CO 80301

187. Suchman, Edward A. (1967) "Evaluation Research"; Russell Sage Foundation, New York, pp.61-66

188. The Hindu (2008) "Despite hiccups, NREGA a boon for rural poor"; Sunday, Feb 10, 2008.

189. Tod, James (1839) "Travels in Western India"; W.H. Allen and Company, London.

190. Truman, David (1951) "The Government Process: Political Interests and Public Opinion", Knoff, New York.

191. United Nations Development Programme (1993) "Human Development Report"; UNDP,New York.

192. United Nations Development Programme (2003) "Human Development Report 2003"; Oxford University Press, New York.

193. Van Meter, D. and Van Horn, C.E. (1975) "The Policy Implementation Process: A Conceptual Framework". Administration and Society, 6 (4), pp. 445–88.

194. Vickers, Sir Geoffrey (1983) "The Art of Judgement"; (2nd ed.) Chapman and Hall, London.

195. Webb, E. J D. T. Campbell, R. D.Schwartz and L.Sechrest, (1966) "Unobtrusive Measures: Nonreactive Measures in the Social Sciences" Rand McNally, Chicago.

196. Weiss, C.H. (1972) "Evaluation Research"; Prentice-Hall, Englewood Cliffs.

197. White, L.D. (1955) "Introduction to the Study of Public Administration"; Macmillan Co., New York.

198. Wholey, Joseph. S (1970) "Federal Evaluation Policy"; Washington: Urban Institute

199. Wilson, Woodrow (1887) "The Study of Administration"; Political Science Quarterly; Vol.2.No.2, June.

200. Xun Wu, M.Ramesh, Michael Howlett and Scott Fritzen(2010) "The Public Policy Primer: Managing the Policy Process" Routledge, New York

❑❑❑

Index

■■■